THE REAL STARGATE

THE REAL STARGATE

Spiderwize
Remus House
Coltsfoot Drive
Woodston
Peterborough
PE2 9BF

www.spiderwize.com

A CIP catalogue record for this book is available from the British Library.

The views expressed in this work are solely those of the author and do not necessarily reflect the views of the publisher, and the publisher hereby disclaims any responsibility for them.

ISBN: 978-1-911596-14-1

Book cover designed by Jeff & Thelma Glanville

Printed by Quality Printers (Reading)

THE REAL STARGATE

By Thelma Glanville

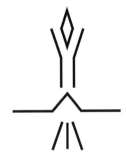

All facts and events are strictly true

Spiritual account of events leading up to a Real Stargate

Location of events: Reading, Berkshire, England

GARTH BOOKS
[Reading]

*Thanks to our immediate family,
human, spiritual and dimensional
friends. May we all one day live together
in peace harmony and understanding
before it's too late!*

Within these pages I have portrayed my loving memories of our spiritual transmission. These memories will stay in my heart forever.

Our learning of the lost knowledge has only just begun; our unconscious minds are just being unlocked. Positive thoughts balanced with the negative and always with love - love is the key.

To experience earthly problems only helps to enrich the soul. We all must learn our lessons to go forth. The teaching of the masters will come.

Many masters from the higher spiritual realm: the councillors, the hooded ones. The love they bestow upon us is great. The full understanding they have of the frail human form and mind. The encouragement given as we stumble along our spiritual pathway. Many doors have and will open. Many pathways set before us. We look to our spirit guides for guidance, but the peace and earthly love comes from within. Find this and you have paradise on earth.

We are our own temples, beings of light, creations of Mother/God.

Just ask and the love with the understanding will be given free with flowing abundance, like a mountain stream cascading down from the heavens. Clear, refreshing, uplifting and, just like that mountain stream, pure, clean, and giving you the pure spiritual truth.

The truth with the love that you will receive will then set you free. Love is all! Love is all! Love is the Key!

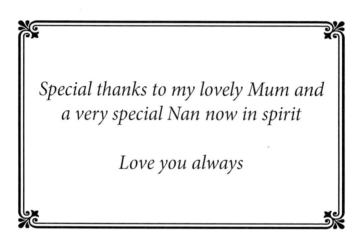

Special thanks to my lovely Mum and a very special Nan now in spirit

Love you always

CONTENTS

The Real Stargate III

Earth Plain VIII

Symbols IX

Meaning To Symbols IX

1.   Saints Preserve Us.. 1

2.   Years Passing 5

3.   At Last A Holiday 7

My Spirit Awakes Poem 12

4.   May - The Awakening 14

5.   Enter Dilys 20

6.   Thursday 16Th May 24

7.   Out Of Control 28

8.   Holy Disaster Night 34

9.   Sideshow 38

10. TG Phone Home Every Day 42

11. Home At Last 46

12. Garden Party 50

13. Show Time And Personal Loss 54

14. Fire! Fire!... 58

15. Great Teaching 72

16. Change Of Direction 80

17. Time To Go Public 85

18. Enlightenment From Our Dimensional Friends 91

19. One Dark And Rainy Night 93

20. Thief In The Night 97

21. A Heavenly Sign In The Sky 103

22. Stargate 12Th October 1996 109

23. Dominic - Higher Realm Spirit 120

24. Wisdom Of The Higher Extra Terrestrials 128

25. The Coming of Our Salvation 130

EARTH PLANE

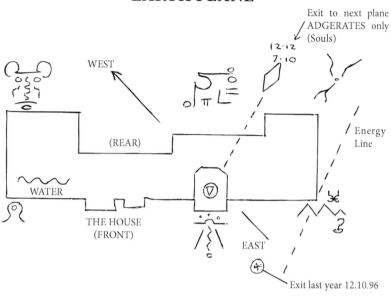

Exit to next plane
ADGERATES only
(Souls)

WEST

12.12
7.10

(REAR)

Energy
Line

WATER

THE HOUSE
(FRONT)

EAST

Exit last year 12.10.96

SYMBOLS

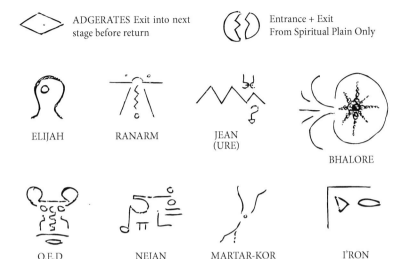

ADGERATES Exit into next stage before return

Entrance + Exit
From Spiritual Plain Only

ELIJAH   RANARM   JEAN (URE)   BHALORE

Q.E.D   NEJAN   MARTAR-KOR   I'RON

Every Spirit has Balance
Bhalore Pure Negativity

MEANING TO SYMBOLS

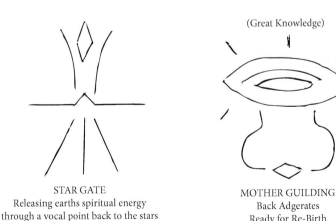

(Great Knowledge)

STAR GATE
Releasing earths spiritual energy
through a vocal point back to the stars

MOTHER GUILDING
Back Adgerates
Ready for Re-Birth

Three Symbols for this lifes code.

 Life Forms Dimention (Negative)
Bhalore Influences.

 Other Life Forms within our own reach (physical & Mental)
Positive with balance.

 Humans made in harmony with Nature.

 (Any Shape) Means Knowledge.

 Return back through to Astral plane.

 Re-entry back to a new life (Re-Birth).

 Position Markers.

X

Directional Markers.

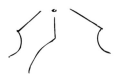

Unlock Sub-conscious information regarding survival &
preparation for catastrophe of future events.
Spiritual awakening for safe return in CHAOS. Etc.
(Not yet unlocked)

Spiritual Awakening.

Spirit Guide.

Energy Crystal converts light into energy creating high vibration.

Dimensional Gateway

Buried Instrument of great power still activated by light source.

XI

Knowledge locked beneath water mass on our plain from a Lost World

Crystal in high vibration formed by light. Opens Dimensional Gateway.

Aliens give knowledge to those who use their Hearts.
(Knowledge Abused)
Aliens also have Adgerates.

Knowledge yet to be discovered?

Have you ever seen an Angel? Have you ever spoken to an Angel? Have you ever had one speak to you?

I have. His name is Jean.

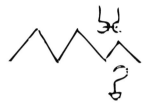

Jean (Ure)

A true spiritual adventure: experiencing a Real Stargate.

I do believe, at the start of things, that it was a haunting. Unknown to us the spirits were giving us an interview. A haunting was 'set up' for us to be spiritually 'sorted out' - literally a test of strength, courage faith and, above all, trust in their powers.

The power of the mind connected to the heart is awesome. The spirit we carry within us is our strength. We are all connected through spirit, given to us by Mother/God. Without us knowing, the spirits guided, protected, loved and backed off each time the pressure was too great through our necessary ordeal. As a family we coped and with the help of our good and faithful new and old friends.

The events that are about to be told are true. It comes from the hearts of all involved. We have laughed, cried and rejoiced together, and come through to greater spiritual rewards. I do believe the time will come when mankind will again obtain the lost knowledge through spiritual awareness, which is vital for our survival on this planet. The questions - all of our whys - will be answered. There is a spiritual battle in progress and Mother/God must and will be the victor. Good and evil, positive and negative - the balance must be corrected and time is short.

I sincerely believe that this is the reason why so many of us are receiving spirit, just like my family and I did on that very special day, Wednesday 15th May 1996, with the interventional help of our dimensional, extra terrestrial friends, of course.

Faith is the substance of things hoped for,
the evidence of things not seen.
Hebrew Verse 11:1

Before we start

On our spiritual path

We must open up our hearts

To things that are true

That come into our lives

And no matter who!

Through thick and thin

We stay to the end

To bring the conclusion

That life will start anew

Thelma Glanville

CHAPTER 1
SAINTS PRESERVE US

Lights and explosions from the skies falling through the trees with great velocity, leaving no smell, vapour or debris. In fact, no evidence at all!

This is what my family and I witnessed in early-October in the year of 1987, with a repeat performance in 1988. 7.30pm on the dot like some invisible hand had thrown a switch. No one daring to venture out to investigate, watching from the safety of our home until it had subsided.

Innocent lights, falling from the heavens. Fooling us all. Turning into something from hell. Crashing, exploding, falling with great speed into the garden. Some impacting mid stream, giving the most weird but wondrous displays. Streams of light piercing the darkness, lighting up the garden as if it was day. Hour upon hour it rained chaos. We were under siege, but from whom?

Each night we sat and waited for the war zone to start. Looking at the clock - bang on 7.30pm Over the following weeks the situation became quite intolerable and distressful for us all, for we had no explanation for this intrusion.

We turned to the local police for help and some sort of guidance. With lashings of tea we sat and tried to explain our situation to two burley coppers. Lured into a false sense of security we relaxed and chatter gave way to laughter, but all too soon the tension was back. Loud and crashing, World War II had returned.

Grabbing their helmets they took flight running out into the front garden, chasing invisible people and sometimes themselves - in and out of the trees shouting instructions, ducking and diving trying to avoid the imaginary bombs that were falling over their heads. What a ringside seat we had peering out from our windows.

Finally, cease-fire. Sheepish, they emerged from the bushes, removing their helmets and scratching their heads. They stood for a while to gain their composure, looking up into the dark skies above, hoping for some answers. It soon became apparent that nothing had been found. Nothing solved. As they took their leave and tried very hard to reassure us not to worry, our morale was at a low ebb.

Frustrated and damn well fed up, we hatched a family plan to capture the pranksters. Our detached house is situated on the old main A4 road, London to Bath, and opposite a private college.

Yes! It has to be some of the students (now grasping at straws). *No other explanation! Why didn't we think of this before?*

Armed with two-way radios, we strategically placed ourselves around the garden and laid in wait. We were ready to take on anybody who dared to venture into our domain. All day we waited and waited to no avail. We found nothing!

The last of the explosions, as I recall again, occurred in mid-October and, of course, at 7.30pm precisely. It seemed to hit the wall just outside the window of the den where I was sitting alone. So loud and so bright that it lit up the room through the heavy closed curtains. Jumping to my feet, I immediately flung open the window, wanting to find something. Surely it had scorched the wall or damaged the plants, but, again, nothing!

The strangest thing, on reflection, was the realization that our surrounding neighbours never complained of these disturbances.

Why haven't they heard the explosions? What a mystery to be solved!

"The power of the visible is the invisible"
Marianne Moore, American Modernist Poet
(1887-1972)

Distant memories of the past

Fly from our minds

Oh so fast

Until one day

They start to creep

To set the scene

To light the fire

Within our hearts

Thelma Glanville

CHAPTER 2
YEARS PASSING

Over the next few years, being a normal, busy family, we put these experiences behind us and simply got on with our lives.

As a mother of two teenage boys, running a small family business, there never seemed to be enough time for me to relax when at home. The house is quite large, built in the 1930s as a bachelor pad, now converted to a family home giving us ample room and space for us all. We even have the luxury of an indoor swimming pool and gym room. This we built in conjunction with the alterations to the entrance of the house and garages.

We now enter from the rear of the house and the large front garden is just left for the birds and postman! The original garage at the front was converted to a gym room. These alterations seemed to go on forever! At last we decided a break was necessary and further building projects were put on hold, to preserve our sanity.

My dad always said of me that I never chucked the towel in. I never knew the full meaning of this saying, but on reflection of the events that will follow, I bow my head to him with love and understanding of his wisdom.

Household chores at home never ceased and I was not going to let a stranger in the house for reasons I thought were quite normal, but David, my hubby, insisted that I employ a young person to help at home. He finally won the day and reluctantly I agreed.

Believe me, that young girl, though only with us for six weeks, had every obstacle put in her way. For some unknown reason, she was not welcome in our home. Everything she touched seemed to be jinxed. She was blamed for rearranging the house, losing things for days on end and burning the dinner, despite being in attendance the whole time while preparing the food. Many a pan was discarded due to its blackened bottom. The poor girl was so confused and we were too! She finally left and things seemed to get back to normal.

Life became very hectic; business was good and time just flew. Very little time was spent together as a family except for holidays. Clearing up after two young boys and our family dog Ben (love him) and, of course, hubby David was not a labour of love. So when I came across balanced objects and furniture moved around, I thought the kids were making a protest or having a little joke on me. Perhaps this was the same for our young girl. Yes! Of course that was the answer.

So I just laughed to myself, put everything back in order and never thought to mention it to anyone, until one day when David came home to find a weird sight in the pool area: It was a balanced tube from the vacuum cleaner with a bucket on top, all standing on an uneven surface. David tried several times to copy without success.

Still not opening our eyes to these events we started to blame each other. God! We must have been so thick-skinned in these early stages of our spiritual awakening; it now makes me feel so sad.

One morning I came running downstairs and on the twist of the staircase stands my lovely figure of a monk reading his prayer book. I always pat his baldhead and wish him "good morning", but this morning he was gone; only the imprint in the stair carpet was visible.

"OK," I shouted, "Who's taken Old Tuck?"

Silence fell through the house. Opening the lounge door, there he stood so proud in the middle of the room. This was getting beyond a joke, as I like my house in order.

Would no one own up to these practical jokes? It was time to stop all this messing around.

CHAPTER 3
AT LAST A HOLIDAY

1996 April Easter weekend - at last a holiday! I insisted that David take me to York and Whitley Bay. It had been a thing of mine for a very long time. I think it was not only the obvious history of the place, but Count Dracula's Castle. The old abbey ruins, which stands on the windswept cliff top overlooking the North Sea. The film had made the place famous and there was a following and a certain attraction for me, as I'm a great fan.

Whitley Bay was rough and exposed to the North Sea, but beautiful in its rawness. Some of our oldest friends decided to come with us. Enjoying the holiday very much, visiting the surrounding areas and staying in some lovely bed and breakfasts, laughter was on the menu until we reached York.

York City was full of tourists like us. The place seemed to shout at me.

Look! See the blood spilt here! The injustice! The murder that took place!

My head swam. What were these strange unexplained disturbing feelings? The place seemed to be asking me to forgive all the persecutors. I found myself looking at a small round tower situated on a mound, with many steps leading up to the gateway. The whole bank was covered in daffodils. What a glorious sight to behold, yet I had this awful overwhelming fear of horror and death. These awesome feelings deep within me were shouting to be free.

I must and will revisit this place again.

I knew this in my heart. The tower I refer to is Clifford's Tower where the persecuted Jews of the city fled for safety, only to be all burnt alive. God have mercy on their souls.

The holiday continued in this strange mood. Thinking we were in good company, we decided to open up and to share our feelings and discuss the strange experiences at home, but to our total dismay we were given the cold shoulder.

This was quite upsetting and disturbing, as these two people had been our friends for so many years and knew we were both uncomplicated people, I would even say down to earth, why such disbelief? David again tried very hard to convince them that things at home were strange, but they were not amused to say the least.

I insisted that to enjoy the rest of the holiday David should keep his thoughts to himself. He promised, but it was so hard as his character compels him to inform.

The last few days were spent visiting antique shops, churches and of course the local pubs. Nothing more was said on the matter. We parted as friends, but during that holiday, David and I had already ventured into unknown territory and had grown apart from them spiritually. This would become painfully obvious due to the forthcoming events.

We finally returned home, feeling a bit dejected, but quite ready to return to work and the family.

Thoughts of home: *How were the boys? The state of the house - clean and tidy I hope. Had the dog been fed or had he gone walkies again?* Ben had the tendency to wander off for days at his own leisure.

My youngest son, Nick, had stayed at home with his cousin Darren. My eldest son, Jeff, had stayed with friends.

Ha! Jeff's away, we shall play, thought Nick. *Lovely. Jeff's hi-fi equipment. Gym equipment yes! Let's have a go.* What a wonderful time you can have when mum, dad, and big brother are away. Let me reassure you that my Nick was old enough to stay at home and be responsible!

The gym is situated next to the den where I was sitting alone on the night of the last explosion. Well, on entering this room, I stood back with shock and horror. Looking up, to my amazement, I saw the heavy exercise bar was balancing on top. I was furious!

This could be dangerous and this was going to be the end of the practical jokes - *look out our Nick* - I was on the warpath. It took two of us to safely take it down.

On tackling my Nick and Darren, they just stood there looking puzzled and their attitude was of one complete denial. They walked off shrugging their shoulders, but their backward glances made me start to think deeply of these strange and unexplained events.

If not Nick or Darren, who or what had done this and why?

"I saw the heavy exercise bar was balancing on the top I was furious!

Abbey Ruins, Whitley Bay

Taurus (April 21 - May 21) - When you have eliminated the impossible, whatever remains, however improbable, must be the truth. Arthur Conan Doyle put those words into the mouth of Sherlock Holmes over a century ago. They apply perfectly to the mystery you are trying to solve. There is a solution to the perplexing dilemma before you. It's not obvious, indeed it requires some real inventive, creative thought to find it. Nonetheless, if you keep your wits about you, you'll see a brilliant answer soon. (May 13th 1996)

Printed in the Hull Daily Mail - Thelma Glanville's horoscope for her 50th birthday in 1996 - very apt indeed!

Positive thinking, smooth flow.

Inspired by our spiritual table

MY SPIRIT AWAKES

The flower unfolds
Each petal at a time
Until it forms
The story to be told
My spirit awakes
At last the dawn breaks
Eyes wide open
Now can see the light
See what is right
Enhance the love
Enhance the day
Now can see the colours array
My spirit awakes
To raise the vibration
To seek the true communication
To be connected
To Heaven and Earth
To see the world with lightened heights
Has given me new birth
To give back to its people
God's great wisdom
In spiritual form
Now knowing
No need to morn
For all my passing loves
Knowing one day
We shall again meet them all
Blessed with the greatest of gifts, unconditional love
For me spirit rules!

Thelma Glanville

While restful thoughts of far away

In the garden where I play

A blast from the past

Came to me on 50th birthday

Came to change our lives forever

    At last!

On that beautiful spiritual 'May Day'

Thelma Glanville

CHAPTER 4
MAY - THE AWAKENING 1996

May was approaching and my thoughts turned to my 50th Birthday. The depths of despair set in and on that dreaded day, I cried and was totally inconsolable. Even when I found my conservatory filled with flowers and cards from my lovely family, I still cried.

On arriving at work I was greeted by my friend Pauline, who had transformed my office with an array of party decorations and presented me with a large birthday cake, but even she could not lift my spirits.

Monday 13th May could not go fast enough for me. It was awful and yet I really did not know why.

I must learn to grow old gracefully. Tuesday came and went. *Carry on as normal*, I thought. *So what. Nobody can escape the marching of time.*

Wednesday the 15th - the weather for May was quite dry. Being a keen gardener I ventured out after dinner - my escape from the house. David had a late evening appointment and my Nick went to visit his Nan, leaving Jeff and I home alone.

That evening I will remember until the day I die. It was the real start of things to come.

I was totally relaxed and absorbed in the job at hand, carefully sprinkling the small border flowers and wrapped up in my own little world, dreaming of all kinds of things, taking time to smell the sweet smelling flowers that had intertwined with the Virginia creeper that clings to the walls of the house and creeps slowly over the roof, like an arm being placed around your shoulder - comforting you.

Then, sharply and abruptly, Jeff's voice came crashing into my world shouting at me with great frustration. Looking up, I saw Jeff's head appearing around the half opened kitchen door directly in line with the gym.

"For God's sake Mum, what do you want me for? You know I'm working out."

He sounded very irritated. Jeff had been working out in the gym for a few weeks trying to turn himself into Mr Universe, and that evening he was following a very hard program. Sweat pouring, his temper and stress levels were very high. For me to interrupt was annoying for him, but I was not guilty. I had not called him at all. He insisted I had called him two to three times and it had sounded very urgent indeed. We were both puzzled. Jeff soon disappeared back to gym mumbling to himself. I carried on watering thinking *how strange.*

Almost immediately the air around me changed. I felt a presence. Oh my God! Something or someone was standing right beside me. Feeling the breath on my face, the loud sigh in my ear expressing such frustration. Wanting to run, but frozen to the spot. Then directly over my head came a very loud crackling noise like a bird flying and swooping, which made me stumble, nearly hitting the ground, but still clutching the water hose. I slowly lifted my head, my eyes searching the garden with great concern and then my attention was drawn to the house.

My whole body feeling like jelly, I struggled to reach the back porch. Peering in the doorway with caution, I wondered what I would find. To my amazement, the shoes which had been neatly placed on the shoe rack just inside the porch, had been thrown everywhere.

Our large, heavy, pine breakfast table has been pushed to one side, trapping all the chairs underneath like someone or something had lost its temper or was very frustrated and needed instant attention. This had been done with such great force.

On seeing this and coming to my senses, I immediately went into the gym, shouting at Jeff, "What the hell's going on?", my eyes raging as I was really spooked and utterly confused.

I blamed him as he did me for calling him earlier. Shouting at Jeff helped me to come back to earth, as I again felt weird and somewhat lightheaded on entering the gym. Well! We both stood there in silence and looked at each other.

David and Nick arrived home together shortly after this incident. Tripping over the shoes and feeling quite puzzled, David called out to us.

"Hello we're home." On realising that Jeff and I were sitting quietly in the sunroom, he continued, "Oh, there you are. What's happened? What's with all the shoes and the table?"

Sitting them down, I poured David a stiff drink and a second for me, and went through the whole episode again, this time with great excitement and relief as we thought that was the end of matter.

David was hanging on every word, but I noticed my Nick was very relaxed and not a bit interested, which I thought was a bit odd! There were the three of us wide-eyed and totally absorbed, while Nick just dismissed it and then totally changed the subject by asking me for an AA book for his car. This I was reluctant to find, as it brought me back to reality, but I did oblige him and went about looking for it, leaving David and Jeff still trying to make sense of the incident.

I searched the den, dining room and so on. It was nowhere to be found. Then someone, a voice in my head, clearly commanded me to look in the lounge.

A voice in my head! What next?

On entering the room, I felt a slight chill in the air. Clutching my body for warmth, I peered into the semi-darkness. To my astonishment I was greeted with the sound of very loud ticking, like the room was filled with clocks. *What!* This was impossible, for I never wind up the clocks, and two of them don't work anyway. On looking around the room, I heard a clear voice say, "carriage clock". I immediately looked at the shelf where the clock had sat. It had gone!

Upon this discovery, the ticking immediately stopped, silence fell, the air changed like I had broken a spell.

"David," I shouted, without really thinking, "Someone has stolen our clock."

It was a beautiful, hand-made French carriage clock David had brought me for a past birthday present, so I was very upset. With this discovery we ran through the house, forgetting all about Nick's book, to check other rooms. On entering one of the spare bedrooms (the green room), we found that the bedclothes were standing upright and beautifully interwoven, shaped like pyramids, standing there so proud.

As we stood back to look upon this amazing sight, David's attitude turned from intrigue to rage within an instant. Pulling and tugging at the covers, he shouted, "Who's responsible for this? I'm not having this in my house."

He has always regretted this action, as a photograph of these wondrous shapes would have been evidence of some mysterious hands at work. Chaos seemed to rain over us. The anger and confusion we felt was very disturbing. What had entered our home and what did it want of us?

Eventually, we said goodnight and tried to settle for some sleep, which was quite a difficult task as our minds and hearts were racing - things in the house were not settled. Laying my head on the pillow, my eyes fell upon a small wicker corner table.

"Oh my God," I screamed.

"What now?" David bellowed.

"David, I put that wicker table up into the loft four weeks ago and now look! Someone has placed it over there in the far corner."

Catching my breath, my eyes frantically searched the bedroom.

There it stood, as bold as brass, with an old china pot plonked on the top. It looked strange and very out of place - just another reminder of the urgent attention needed, but by whom?

Cold shivers went through me and sleep that night was impossible. My side light stayed on all night and for many nights to come. Without our knowing, these unexplained events had already changed our lives forever.

We will not know unless we begin.
Howard Zinn, American Historian, Playwright and Social activist (1922-2010)

From the family comes a helper

To sort out ones dilemma

To find the cause

To bring fourth

A spiritual adventure

Thelma Glanville

CHAPTER 5
ENTER DILYS

With great excitement, I phoned my sister, Dilys, who always had time to listen and help me with most of my problems.

To my amazement, she was very laid back and simply stated, "It seems that you have a visitor." She said she would call to see us on Thursday night - 16th May.

I am the youngest of four sisters and Dilys, Dil for short, is the second youngest. We became very close after the loss of her only son Matthew who died on his 21st birthday of testicular cancer - a tragic loss to us all. How can a mother bear such pain? How cruel life can be. Not forgetting her husband who to this day cannot express his true feelings without tears. My loving thoughts are always with them both and, of course, their daughter.

Our upbringing was Church of England. Sunday school and bible classes were in order until the other things took their place. Our parents were not strict about religion, but did bestow upon us truth, goodness and honesty. My father had been a Sergeant Major in the army and suffered not only physical but mental pain. The stories that he told us of the Second World War were too much to bear. He was dedicated to King and Country, yet always stated that any war is wrong, but sometimes necessary. Our dad is no longer with us, yet we will go on loving him until we all can be reunited. As my mum says: "Until the dawn breaks".

Our mum, bless her, is a little Welsh lady and, without her, my Nick would be totally lost. Down to earth and full of life, though well over 80 years of age, she can 'jump over our heads' at any time (her favourite saying). She's great our mum. Fools she will not suffer lightly and she has no qualms in telling you so.

After the loss of Matthew, Dilys felt the need to visit a local medium, who had an excellent reputation. Although it did not concur with our family beliefs, we accepted this as it seemed to give her great comfort. I accepted it as being the right thing for Dilys, but I would never have considered visiting such a lady! My thoughts and beliefs were quite different. Following the bible code, you do not speak to the dead, they cannot speak to you, and I was quite convinced of that fact. Yet I did respect other people's views and beliefs.

Dil's visits to this lady became less and less. Obviously time is a great healer and Dil had stated that Matthew had visited her at home and they had held their own conversations. Well, she's my sister and this was OK with me. As I said, her visits grew less frequent while Dil herself grew stronger spiritually. The courage she showed over the years was remarkable, and she seemed to come to terms with the death of her son.

Many times he had visited her in dreams and took her to a place of learning.

He told her, "Please don't wish me back Mum. I am so happy doing the job chosen for me. Please don't worry about me."

Without knowing, my sister was becoming a medium herself with the help of her loving son. This would soon become apparent to us all.

What we anticipate seldom occurs: but what we least expect generally happens.
Benjamin Disraeli, British Politician, Writer and Prime Minister (1804-1881)

Open up the hearts and minds

To feel the energy divine

Filled with love

From above

To accept and understand

The contact of spirit

From a very 'special unique man'

Thelma Glanville

CHAPTER 6
THURSDAY 16TH MAY

Thursday, 6.30pm - no time for dinner; just a snack. Still the excitement was very high. Sitting on the phone all day telling friends that we had spirits in the house seemed quite novel to us all, but little did we know!

David was again busy with appointments that evening, but waited for the arrival of Dilys. As soon as we heard her car on the drive we ran out to meet her, all talking at once, going through the whole episode over and over again. Finally, we sat down in the conservatory with a tray full of goodies, as the temperature seemed to have dropped in the main part of the house and felt quite chilly. Casually, Dil mentioned that she would like to stroll around the house.

"Where was your clock Thelma?" she asked.

"In the lounge," I replied. With that information she disappeared off in that direction.

"I really must go now love or I will be late," said David.

Just then we heard my sister shout with great urgency, "Thelma come quick."

My Nick looked at me and said, "I'm off Mum. I'm not staying here, no way." He laughed nervously and disappeared out the back door.

David, Jeff and I immediately ran into the lounge, now icy cold, only to find Dil transfixed, standing by the fireplace, holding her hands up in the air.

"I cannot move. There is someone here stopping me, and I feel he or she is holding my hands."

I looked at David and Jeff with wonderment.

"Are you having us on Dil?" I asked seriously, for I had never ever witnessed this kind of thing before, and certainly not from one of my sisters.

She started to cry uncontrollably; the tears fell with emotion.

"Oh God Dil. What's wrong?" I asked, not knowing what to do, frightened even to touch her. "Jeff, go and make her a cup of tea."

Tea is always the answer. We just stood there like lemons and stared at her, still crying. David, by this time, was very late but didn't want to leave us. He was very concerned, not fully comprehending the situation, but on my reassurance that we could cope, he left.

I was then left on my own with Dil, and I gently coaxed her to sit on the chair, which finally she did and her crying seemed to cease.

All this time she seemed to be in a semi-trance, her eyes quite glazed and an awful faraway look on her face, which made me worried.

"Dil can you hear me?" I asked, speaking very softly to her, "Dil, it's me Thelma."

I slipped my hand into hers, trying to give her some comfort. *Hurry up with that tea Jeff,* I thought.

Well, I should never have done this, as it was a very wrong move indeed! The only way I can describe the pain, shock and horror of the moment is to liken it to placing one's body on an electric chair. Like an empty cup, my body filled up with an electrical charge, head to foot. My eyes bulged and my body increased in size, and I seemed to be lifted up. Looking up towards the ceiling, with great strength, I let out the most horrifying scream, so loud and piercing that it jolted Dilys out of her trance and made Jeff fly from the kitchen. Jeff immediately placed his arm around my neck to stop me falling backwards. Dilys also took hold and they both tried to calm me down. My whole body was taken over with horror and fear. What was I witnessing?

"Mum, Mum," Jeff screamed with fright, "What bloody well happened to you? I thought you were both being murdered."

My heart was pounding. My mind and body were not my own!

"We have got to get out of this room. Someone or something is very sad and unhappy," said Dil now fully aware of her faculties.

We wasted no time and fled into the den, thinking it would go away - whatever it was! We sat there wide-eyed and just looked at each other, all trying to catch our breath.

"Oh my God," Dil yelled, "It's followed us. It's in here again." The coldness filled the room, the air changed. "Look at Jeff!"

I started to scream again. Jeff's eyes were bulging, just like mine had. His body stiffened and he went into a trance like state. We were again terrified.

"Jeff, Jeff!' I cried, "Please don't hurt my son. Let him go."

I was not sure who or what I was screaming at. Jeff then started to fight against the power that had possessed him, his arms and legs thrashing around uncontrollably. By this time, he had demolished my glass coffee table, kicking away the whole damn support. It took all our strength to hold him down and bring him back to reality.

That night Dilys, Jeff and I not only received spirit, but also witnessed a whole episode of bizarre events. Immediately after Jeff had recovered from his ordeal, we were greeted with a strong, overwhelming smell of wood smoke that filled the kitchen. Beautiful, blue, curly smoke wafted up from nowhere. Items appeared on walls, which I had packed away months ago after decorating. An Egyptian head of Queen Nefertitii was placed very neatly on the wall in the kitchen, replacing my small china sun, which had been placed in the hanging brass pot. We didn't know that evening, that these things were to become the key to the unfolding spiritual events.

Help was needed and fast, not only for us three, but also for the lonely, trapped and distressed spirit that walked our house. At last it had made contact, its salvation at hand.

"Sun" appeared over area where "back door" used to be in kitchen to represent "Insurance farfine".

Egyptian Head appeared on wall after 1st visit by spirit & trance in kitchen.

Go with the heart. Worry not the mind.
Inspired by our spiritual table

CHAPTER 7
OUT OF CONTROL

During the weeks that followed, the events within the house went from bad to worse. Each night when we arrived home from work it was waiting, like it had heard us at the gate, the key in the latch, and as soon as we entered it greeted us.

Let me describe the feeling of a spirit so desperate for human contact: First intense tingling, light headedness and wooziness. Then there's the pressure that comes with the full force of its presence within you. Your whole being is forced back into your body and the spirit manifests through. The desperation of the first time it speaks through your own throat. Your eyes are shut, yet you can see. Movements of your body - wild and uncontrollable. The sudden attacks of diarrhoea that make you fly to the bathroom with the energy the spirit produces.

All this I experienced. Jeff seemed to have gained more control in resisting the spirit's advances. Although we had now witnessed the spirit manifesting in this fashion, David and I had not grasped the situation or the true meaning of this spiritual contact. Obviously very upset to see me in this state and at his wits' end, he decided to seek professional help.

Meanwhile, in the midst of all this havoc, we overlooked our gardener, named John, who called to the house on a regular basis to cut the grass and keep the trees and bushes in order. One morning I caught John in the front garden looking at a very funny sight indeed!

"It looks like someone has been trying to enter your dining room through the foliage," he said laughing as he inspected a funny little tunnel that weaved in and out of the foliage.

What was funny about that? I thought.

"No, you don't understand. It's nothing to worry about, it's spiritual," he carried on, still laughing to himself. John is very jolly and likes a good natter, but he's also very wise in an old sort of way.

"'Spiritual'? What do you mean?" I said, looking at him with intense eyes.

"You have a lot of energy in the garden, especially in certain areas," he said, now quite serious.

"What do you know about such things?" I enquired.

"My mother is a medium and I grew up learning all about the spiritual world. You have enormous amounts of electrical energy building up. If I pick up any further information today, I'll pop in your office - OK?" he said.

"Did David tell you about the problems we're having in the house?" I replied with great relief.

"Yes! Fully understand. I'll speak to you later." With that he carried on gardening.

Well! This was a turn up for the books: a psychic gardener.

"No John. You've got to come into the house with me now," I said, tears now falling. "It's very important, please."

Following me into the house, we both entered the breakfast room. He started to shake his head.

"God I feel very light headed and someone is following me, and I can hear a clock ticking very loud, but I cannot see where it's coming from. Phew that's enough for me. As I said, I'll call in to see you later at the office. And don't worry," he said with a reassuring voice.

Do not worry! I was going out of my mind!

At 2.00pm on the dot he arrived, still very chatty and laid back.

"There you are. This is what I picked up spiritually when you left me this morning."

He handed me a list on which he'd written:

18TH CENTURY - FIRE
French man very tall dressed in 18th century dress (tunic / white shirt / wide like Quaker collar / tall hat / buckle shoes) Egypt scholar / French books named him Jean-Louis. Does not like shoes and we have something of his he would like returned.

Well thanks John, I thought. As if I didn't have enough troubles. He laughed.

"Bye. Don't worry. He's not there to harm you. I'll see you in the week. Please keep me informed and ring me if you need any help. Bye." he said, giving me a big grin. On this, he disappeared through the door, leaving me even more confused.

Well finally David made contact with two elderly ladies from the spiritualist church who called one sunny afternoon in late May. We all sat in the garden and gave them complete freedom of the house to explore. The house is late 1930s, but the site, as I stated before, was on the old A4 road, London to Bath. Surely there had been some wicked, dark deeds done up and down this domain. It had been said that Dick Turpin had ridden this highway, and the War of the Roses had been fought at Newbury and the surrounding areas from 1455-1487. Then there was Cromwell's army that hid at Mapledurham on the other side of the river Thames. Yes, this road is steeped in history, and the site - what of the site itself? The mind boggles!

Stage coach to represent "Jean" pulling up to
Inn where he stayed & met his fate.

David, Dil, Jeff and I just sat there in the garden, sipping our tea in complete silence, waiting for the ladies to appear. The day was lovely:

birds singing, garden looking nice and neat, and certainly not a day for spooks at all. Had it all been a dream?

Suddenly one of the ladies, Winnie I think, flew out the back door and shouted to her colleague. Mavis appeared from the window of the back bedroom, which we call the blue room. Her face was filled with great excitement, Winnie ran back into the house. They seemed to be concentrating on one part of the house. It seemed a lifetime before they finally emerged and rejoined us in the garden. They both looked very pleased with themselves.

"Well you certainly have a spirit in the house. I saw him standing in the dining room and he walks the house in a certain pattern," Mavis said smiling. To our amazement she started to describe the man just like John did. "Fire, yes, there is evidence of a great fire. I smelt wood smoke. This man is not here to harm you. We shall arrange to call back one evening and pass him over to the light," she said, so matter-of-factly, like we knew what "passing over to the light" meant!

On leaving, Mavis gave us all a grim warning!

"You must learn to shut down. Do not allow spirits to enter at will. You have no control or protection." Her tone was now quite serious. "Batten down the hatches," she carried on, putting her arm around me giving me a squeeze. "Learn to use your Chakras. Be a good girl."

Good advice, I'm sure. Well, we knew nothing of these things, and Mavis did not have time to fully explain the whole concept of the spiritual world, but over the next few months, we were to learn it all through other ways and means, as time was running out for our spirit that walked the house.

Time went by. The ladies from the church did not return, even when we chased them up - nothing. Things were now getting desperate at home, especially with me. I was still receiving spirits and could not shut down as advised. I had no idea what was expected of me. The spiritual force that had now entered me emerged as an Italian lady that had complete control. I was now singing Italian Opera. Italian! Yet I knew not one word.

I was screaming, crying, asking to be forgiven, even blaspheming. Within these rages, and when this spirit was very strong, furniture would move around the house, especially in our green bedroom just at the top of the stairs overlooking the front garden. The furniture in this room would be thrown around and turned upside down like someone or something was searching. This seemed to happen in the same corner each time she came to me.

One night, I found myself standing at the bottom of the staircase, looking up into our beautiful stained glass window above the half landing, which extends to the full height of the staircase. There she was, waiting for me. I knelt down, looking up with eyes full of pain, my heart crying out for forgiveness. She entered me once again.

Transfixed by the window, it had now become an altar to her. The heavy wooden frame had formed a cross. A head of a wall ornament had been placed at the top of the cross, and was now looking down at me like Jesus. With this image, I flung myself down on the stairs, waving my arms, shouting out once again in Italian. I knew in my heart she was so desperate to be forgiven, but what awful crime had she committed?

I was totally out of control. I had become a mad woman. Exhausted and weak from the constant diarrhoea attacks caused by the spiritual energy in the house and the Italian lady entering me at will, and with no sign of help coming from the spiritual ladies, David turned to the conventional church.

Our beautiful stained glass window looking like Jesus on the cross

Singing once again, oh so loud

Came the Italian lady without a break

To perform once again

To everyone in her wake

Scattering our visitor on that day

That came to help

But afraid and did not stay

Thelma Glanville

CHAPTER 8
HOLY DISASTER NIGHT

Within days of Mavis's visit, David arranged for our local vicar to call on Wednesday night. Gathering together, we sat in the dining room. Hearing his knock on the door, I quietly asked David to let him in, as I was not up to greeting him the way I should. I had lost my voice due to the very loud singing of the Italian lady.

He was a young vicar and he had no experience of what he was about to witness. Offering him a cup of tea, we tried to settle down to his long-awaited talk, which we thought would solve all our problems. Sitting there and trying very hard to listen to his words of wisdom, the air was changing around us.

Dil looked at me with wide eyes and mouthed the words, "Can you feel it?"

The cold was swirling around our legs like a snake coming up from the earth. I froze to the spot and said nothing. The vicar went on talking about our "little problem" as he called it, and suggested that we kept a daily diary of the events to see if a pattern formed, which we all agreed was a very good idea. Still chatting, I gave David a sign to take the vicar on a tour of the house and give him more insight into our dilemma, not wanting to put him on the spot, as the spirit around us was now very strong indeed. It took all my strength and courage to hold her back.

"Dilys, help me please. I feel her so strong."

I struggled to get the words out and feared the worst. By this time, David, Jeff and the vicar had reached the top of the stairs near the green bedroom. They called to us both to join them. Dil and I mounted the stairs reluctantly. Looking at each other, we felt the cold and tingles engulfing us once again. In full trance I took flight and performed for the vicar. The vicar stood there in shock.

"Bless me Father, for I must be possessed," I cried, struggling to come out of the trance that held me in bondage. By this time I was on bent knees. His hand barely touched my head, as he repeated the Lord's Prayer, his voice a whisper. With this blessing, he flew down the stairs, hurriedly talking to David.

"I'll be back with some of my colleagues who have more understanding and knowledge of these matters," he promised.

With his last words ringing in our ears, he left. We were alone again to pick up the pieces, feeling empty and with nowhere to go, asking ourselves who we should turn to next?

Destiny is not matter of chance. It is a matter of choice.
William Jennings Bryan, Former US Secretary of State (1860-1925)

Cold are the hearts that are not open

Minds that are closed

Doeth finger point

To things that are shown

Must not condemn

As not their time

To enter the spiritual den

Thelma Glanville

CHAPTER 9
SIDESHOW

The events were ongoing and relentless. All kinds of smells filled the house. Perfume, sweet tobacco, farmyard smells and, of course, the heavy, sickly wood smoke. Furniture continued to move around the house with ease. Bright blue flashes accompanied the movements of wall ornaments; we would spend hours trying to hunt them down, finding them in the most unlikely places. Bright specks of glowing light, which we called stars, fell downwards and rose upwards, especially over people's heads.

We would see strange moving smoke contained in an outer circle that disappeared through the wall between the den and the gym room, beautiful displays on our dining room table and cold spots where you could see your own breath. Sometimes at night I could hear Ben, our family dog, walking around the kitchen; he had become so very restless. We often found him wandering, feeling very lost and resisting our attempts to coax him upstairs. I expect he was also feeling the energy and the tension of our spooks.

Trying to cope with running our business and handling this awful situation was sometimes unbearable. We thought we could share it with some of our old friends and family, but this sometimes made it worse, even

BEN on Boat holiday.

when we showed them the evidence at home. Some of the remarks were quite understandable, but so negative. I suppose if we were unable to grasp the meaning of the situation, then there wasn't much hope for them.

How can you live in a house that's haunted? Aren't you terrified? Can't you just sell up and move on? Let's see something move then.

On inspecting evidence, the usual question was "who did that?", like it was one of us having a lovely game. The worst insult of all was when they did not listen to our plight, when we were bearing our souls, ignoring us and laughing at us.

What a big joke! Avoid them at all cost. Change the subject.

We were becoming a sideshow.

These unexpected reactions hurt us both very much. We were drifting away from some of our friends and nothing could stop it. This affected David. His mood started to change towards us and the situation at home. He got quite angry when Jeff and I received or even felt the presence of the spirit. David, at this time, was unable to share or experience this. Even the movement of furniture was wearing a bit thin.

"Just stand and feel the air open up your heart and let the spirit in," I pleaded, feeling the desperation of the spirit as well as my own.

At one time he accused us of conspiracy. Although we knew we always had his love, his trust was faltering.

Life must go on and, through all this uproar, Jeff still tried to carry on with his program in the gym, but even this pleasure was taken away from him. The gym equipment became useless. Even after a ten minute session the weights would become as light as air. One night Jeff was able to lift the whole apparatus with one hand. Sometimes, during these attempts to train, the spirit would try and take advantage of him. Jeff always resisted and ran out into the garden with great fear. This room was becoming unbearable to him.

I phoned my sister on a regular basis to keep her informed of events. We seemed to obtain a certain psychic link and trance would become very easy and natural for both of us. We had that feeling someone was always listening in on our conversations. Dil thought it would be a good idea if I arranged to visit her medium, as we'd had no further response from the vicar. Perhaps she could shine a light into the darkness for my family and me.

The meeting went very well. Although the medium did not discuss my immediate problem at home, she changed some of my views, as she was correct in all manner of things, especially about my personal life. I was totally amazed. This left me quite calm and, for the first time since all this chaos, quite positive. I felt like me again. I was sure I would meet this lady again, but not as her client. Thanks Dil.

During this time, I had an unexpected visit one early evening while cooking dinner. There was a knock on the back door and in walked the vicar with a senior colleague, completely unannounced. Well, I could not hide my complete surprise, as I thought they had forgotten me just like the spiritual church.

Making them comfortable with some light refreshments, we all sat in the den. They were very polite and quite concerned about what they referred to as "my problem". Good advice was offered as well as an invite to attend the church for counselling at any time. They said that at the end of the day, of course, it was my fault entirely, as I was just a curious sort of person who liked to solve mysteries. I could shut this down at any time. Well, this was partly true, as I believe God has given us all the freedom of choice.

I gave serious thought to their words and decided to go and talk to Mavis from the spiritual church. I rang and made an official appointment. Wednesday, the day of reckoning, came! As I drove to her home, I was mulling things over in my head. Would she remember me? Why did she not return? I would make sure she listened to me today, as I was in right pickle.

Taking a deep breath, I rang the doorbell, preparing myself as best I could, and waited. No one came, so I rang again and this time banged on the door. I was not going away, I had made an appointment and I needed help.

Please be in for me! Please, I pleaded.

I waited an hour for her that day and got a parking ticket in the bargain. She had not forgotten; she was just a busy person. Well, the wait and the hours I spent with Mavis were not wasted. What a wonderful lady - so full of knowledge, wisdom and, above all, so very kind. She apologized over and over again for not returning to our house and she never did, but as you will see, her help was no longer needed. Without really knowing, we had already started out on our own spiritual pathway and were learning more each precious day.

That day she introduced me to my spirit guide: a man from Peru (no name was given). I now know that we have many spirit guides who are always near at hand to provide help, guidance and protection. Thanks Mavis.

CHAPTER 10
TG PHONE HOME EVERY DAY

It was mid-June and we certainly needed a holiday away from it all: office, home and spirits. David, being a boat lover, arranged a week's holiday with two old friends. Falmouth to Plymouth was on the menu. Great! David and I were looking forward to this break. We needed it so much to recuperate and get back on track.

At that time we owned a small powerboat which could be towed most anywhere. When time allowed, we spent lazy days cruising down the beautiful River Thames. Henley Regatta was a favourite and, of course, the Solent on the south coast.

Ben, our lovely family dog of 18 years, was both our friend and companion on these trips. Throughout this spiritual ordeal, our Ben suffered from the energy in the house. This fact I was sure of. He died on 15th July 1996 after a heart-breaking weekend for reasons that would become apparent.

I was very anxious to ask the boys to stay home and monitor the house, especially my Nick as he was acting very strangely. Was he blocking things out or did he know more than he admitted? He's a lovely lad, but he prefers a one-to-one relationship with me, and sometimes it can be as frustrating to me as it is for him. Finding me nattering on the phone or entertaining any of my friends upsets him. One Saturday, he came home early from work, only to catch me in the kitchen gossiping on the phone.

Popping his head around the half open back door by all the shoes, he caught my eye and whispered to me, "Mum how long are you going to be and who is sitting in the sunroom?"

MY NICK PREFERS TO BE WITH ME ONLY NOT GOOD IN A CROWD.

The expression on my face must have said it all, as I was totally alone in the house. Cutting my conversation short, I immediately investigated. Flinging back the curtains that shield the breakfast room from the sun, I peered in with great expectations, but it was empty! I looked back at my Nick, who had not ventured past the door. He insisted that a man was still sitting in the chair with his books neatly placed on this lap. He described him in full detail as he could see him through the window and I knew he was looking into the face of our Frenchman, Jean-Louis. Finally coaxed Nick in and together we said a small prayer.

It was Friday night the day before our holiday. Preparing for our trip gave me a purpose and, for a short while, it took my mind off our invisible intruders, which seemed to have eased. David and I went to bed early after a busy evening, packing up the boat for an early start. As I previously stated, Jeff had become disillusioned with the gym equipment as it had become light and useless due to the spiritual energy, so he had decided to work out in the pool area. We had been in bed for a few hours, leaving Jeff to enjoy the delights of the swimming pool. Nick had already deserted the house and gone to see his Nan. With David already asleep, I was left with my thoughts. Thinking of the last few months, my head swam trying to make some sense of everything.

What was really going on and why us? Was it all a dream or some kind of a joke? All the things we'd witnessed and experienced - was it all real?

Suddenly, I had this awful feeling welling up inside me. The air had become very cold. Jeff was shouting for me with great fear. Without a moment to lose, like a bat out of hell, I flew down to the pool. What I witnessed I could not believe. It was like something from a horror picture. Jeff was doing sit-ups at a rate not humanly possible. The speed was unreal.

"Help me Mum. I can't stop. There's a force around me."

He was now crying with pain. I immediately spread my hands out into the air. It was like a force field - strong and impregnable.

Raising my hands even higher over his head I said in a very loud and positive voice, "Leave my son. Go back to where you came from and leave now," followed by the Lord's prayer, which I repeated over and over again.

As soon as my words had left my lips the entity, with great disgust, flipped my son up into the air and he somersaulted backwards into the pool. Jeff was left writhing in agony. By this time David was standing at my side.

This was not a dream! This had just become a bloody nightmare. Holiday? After this I did not want to go anywhere. This was going to be the worst week of my life. I needed a protector for the boys while I was away and of course it had to be Dilys. This I would organise.

Reluctantly, we left the next morning for our holiday, as the night had not brought any further disruptions. Kissing and hugging the boys as they tried to reassure us that everything would be all right, the guilt was heavy in my heart as we left that morning.

"Go on Mum. Have a lovely time. I'm feeling much stronger now," Jeff whispered in my ear, trying very hard to convince me.

We had a week of perfect boating with fabulous weather. You cannot beat England when the weather is right. The boat was running smooth with everything falling into place. The coastline from Falmouth to Plymouth is stunning from the water. Each night we would stop at a different harbour and hunt out the bistros offering the gastronomic delights of fresh lobster and crab. Sharing the fun and laughter with our friends on the high seas, walking along the seashore with Ben, and the three of us curling up each night together, as snug as a bug - it was wonderful.

Starting in Falmouth, we took the opportunity to catch up with David's family. David's family all originated from Cornwall. His eccentric grandfather owned the most beautiful mansion in the heart of the only forest in the area, in a small village named Praze-an-beeble. Sadly, this property was sold in the late 60s and the proceeds were split amongst the family after his death. It's now a time-share paradise.

David is one of four brothers. At the age of seven, he tragically lost his mum as the result of a simple error during an operation. His dad, in shock, decided to emigrate to Australia, selling up and taking his young sons to a country very alien to them. They lasted for two years before deciding to come home. Trying very hard to come to terms with his grief, he finally settled in Reading. On his retirement, he decided to return to his roots and now lives in the beautiful coastal town of Penzance.

At every opportunity I would phone home. Thoughts of my boys were never far away. I went into panic each time there was no answer. Finally, I reached my Nick.

"Hello Mum. Having a nice time? What's the weather like? How's Dad?"

He was really pleased to hear from me.

"Yes, yes," I said, very impatiently. I really did not want to talk about my holiday as I was intrigued to know what was going on at home. "What's going on? Everything OK?"

I must have been such a bore as I rattled on. Finally, getting a word in edgeways, he confirmed that Jeff had been hearing noises in the house - air changing around him all the time, footsteps coming along the landing, which seemed to stop at his bedroom door.

"Dil! Have you contacted Dil?" I bellowed down the phone.

I felt so helpless, so far away from home. We arrived at Plymouth our last port of call and our last day at sea. Although we'd had a fantastic time I was glad it was over. Packing up was great; we were on our way home!

1964 Clowance
Praze-An-Beeble Cornwall, David's Grandfather's estate now
a time share paradise also believed to be haunted.
(Me & David's aunty in the background)

CHAPTER 11
HOME AT LAST

On opening the door, the smell of the house was wonderful: welcoming and amazingly quiet and serene. It was like walking into a church - you know - that feeling of wellbeing. The air was fresh and clear. Ben had been around the garden several times and was getting his land legs back. He finally curled up into his basket and fell asleep. He'd had a wonderful holiday - such a loving dog. I ran through the house checking each room. OK. Everything was OK - great. Had it finally gone? Even David agreed it felt different.

The boys. Where were my boys? I was soon on the phone to my mum.

"Yes they're both here," she said. "They'll be home in 10 minutes."

I could not wait. I left David unpacking the boat. I started to prepare the evening meal. Looking up, there they were. Hugs and kisses, even tears. Even Ben woke up to greet them. We called for David and all sat down for a family powwow, talking ten to a dozen, exchanging stories of the week gone by.

Finally, I got the boys to talk about the house.

"It's wonderful. So calm and peaceful and yet I thought you had some awful problems," I said, repeating what Nick had told me.

As soon as I mentioned this, Jeff's facial expression changed.

"Well Mum, there have been few things going on, so we both decided to stay down at Nan's. I suppose that's why the house seems so restful."

My heart grew heavy with this information. There had been no change, just a reprieve. For the things that had happened in the past few months were just the tip of the iceberg. It did not take long for things to return to chaos: furniture being stacked up to the ceiling, balanced in the most precarious way; the house filling up with that sickly wood smoke; stars falling and moving with great ease through the walls.

We were all under a lot of stress. My Nick had virtually left home; his bed was empty most nights. He had complained of noises coming from the void area, which forms part of his bedroom. He would sometimes place a barricade across the small door. The void was only filled with discarded toys from their youth - nothing that would make noises! Yet he insisted the door remain shut at all times. He was so frightened already that we decided not to tell him that we had found his bed flipped over twice!

Jeff was chased along the landing and down the stairs by loud clicking noises, which seem to spark at the same time around his head. The house filled with an electrical charge. Feeling very sick and in an awful state, he looked at me with eyes full of fear and bewilderment.

"It's becoming a nightmare to live here Mum," he whimpered, staring at me, looking for some kind of guidance. Of course I had none to give. I felt I had failed them both. Jeff was right: our home was total bedlam. We had no one to turn to. Had God forsaken us?

Chairs stacked in Gym, moved from dining room.

My Nick's bed flipped over 2 times.
Note: His bed was full of books in the draws - so heavy!

My Nick was called by spirit "Pluto" being the most distant planet in the solar system. He always resisted the whole concept of spiritual contact.

Life shrinks or expands in proportion to one's courage
Anaïs Nin, Essayist
(1903-1977)

CHAPTER 12
GARDEN PARTY

Shortly after our holiday the weather was still lovely and warm. Dil's friend Heather introduced her to John P and his partner Gina. Gina's daughter and Heather's son had just had a beautiful baby girl, so the couple were now part of the family.

Chatting merrily and enjoying the English weather at its best, they all sat out in Gina's garden. Without warning, Dilys went into a trance. There she was, with cup and saucer in hand, groaning and trying very hard to bring the spirit through.

Well! This set the tea party off with a bang.

"Where has this come from?" Gina gasped. She shouted for John P.

Heather had some quick explaining to do about our house and the ongoing phenomena. By this time John P was present. Without any hesitation he quietly spoke to her.

"She's is in deep trance, let her be."

Heather explained things to John P and he was most intrigued. Unbeknown to Dilys, John P was, and still is, a practicing Freemason and since he was a young man, he had been receiving spiritual messages and was very well read up on the subject of spiritualism. What a find! Once again, many thanks Dil.

John P is a real gentleman: polite and well mannered and very kind. With our full permission and to our great relief, he arranged for a meeting to be held at our house one afternoon.

Being fully introduced, we all sat in my garden. David was not present as he'd decided to leave things to me, so I invited my friend Pauline along for moral support.

We talked, laughed and discussed our problem with great ease. Great - at long last someone understood. We seemed to bond straight away and became friends that very day.

Gina was getting rather excited as she could feel the tingles out in the garden.

"Oh John P, let's go in," she said.

"If it's ok with Thelma," John replied. *So polite!*

"What do you intend to do John P?" I asked.

"Well, as I explained, Gina is a very good trance medium and she will pick up the spirit very quickly and see what it wants, for you," he added, reassuring me.

I felt in good hands, but was still a bit nervous about the suggested séance.

We decided the best place for a séance was the dining room where Mavis had first seen our gentleman spirit. On entering, Gina was taken aback by the serenity of the room. It overlooks the front garden so the foliage is kept quite high around the bay. A tall, reed-like plant grows around the base. I think it's a wild weed, but it's very beautiful and gives the room a green glow, especially when the sun shines through its leaves.

Immediately, a robin appeared within its stems. It seemed to peer in at us through the window. This filled my sister's heart with joy as her friend the medium had been told by her son, Matthew, that this would be his symbol on earth when near.

Drawing the curtains, we took our places around the table.

"Can you light a candle and dim the lights as this is beneficial to meditation?" John P said.

We each in turn looked at each other, not knowing what to expect. John was marvellous, controlled and organized. He had apparently done this many times before. This was to become our special room for future spiritual gatherings.

After a short but inspiring prayer, John asked for the love and protection from his spirit guide.

"Bring down the colours, pink for love and blue for healing. Empty your minds of every day burden," were his instructions.

Total peace filled the room. The wall lights were dimmed and one candle was flickering. Utter tranquillity! One eye shut, the other open, I looked around the room. I looked at Gina who had already gone into a trance and was speaking softly, not loud enough for me to hear her words. This went on for a while and we all waited, but nothing happened. Gina slowly came out of her trance.

"Nothing but darkness John," she said.

"Let's give it time. We are here for them," he said lovingly. "Let's be patient."

"Ooooh... It's getting very cold around my feet," Dil said, her voice at a whisper. The air had changed within the room. It was clammy, heavy, thick, as if the room had filled with invisible smoke. Oh my God, I was filling once again like that empty cup. Up, up, up to the brim. My eyes bulging, body puffed up, my head was thrown back so that I was looking directly up to the ceiling towards the green bedroom directly above. I experienced a lifting sensation, feeling like a balloon in flight. Total fear overcame me and I let out that awful piercing scream once again. Then I was crying and cradling an imaginary baby in my arms with great tenderness and love. It was the Italian lady. The guilt she carried in her heart was such a burden. God forgives her for her crime whatever it was-1 was sure of that fact.

Before I knew it, John P had me under control. As he laid his hands on my shoulders, healing hands that penetrated through to my soul, the spirit subsided.

Talking gently and lovingly, he said "It's a memory, let it go."

Slowly I recovered and came to.

"We must meet again to pass this poor soul over to the light. It seems that she is mourning for her lost child," he added.

Eyes blurred and still wiping away the tears, I looked around the room. Pauline was terrified and, to my knowledge, never attended another séance. Gina was flabbergasted. Dilys and Jeff had, of course, witnessed this before. The séance was over.

Instantly, John P and Gina became part of our daily spiritual lives. They became our dear friends, our salvation. Between them they taught us to cope and survive our necessary ordeal.

From that day on, we moved in leaps and bounds. The learning process became fun. Control at last. We started to look forward to our regular séances, not only because we received spirits, but also because of the loving and friendly nature of our meetings.

Jeff was still reluctant and my Nick was nowhere to be found.

David, or "beloved" as the spirits called him, gradually came to terms with our "spooks".

Each meeting was tape-recorded with the help of Heather's husband: a dear man named Albert who had a late calling to our group.

Having establishing our spiritual group with loving friends, we found peace and harmony. Above all, we accepted the invasion of spirits into our home and lives, and thinking we now knew the reason for their presence.

A spiritual leader once said that spirits would sweep you along with gusto unless you told them to slow down.

But Jean was having none of this - time was short and unknowing to us all the gathering of the Stargate had already begun.

CHAPTER 13
SHOW TIME AND PERSONAL LOSS

During our years of business, we sometimes met famous people. The Berkshire area hosts a number of such people: George Harrison, Freddie Star, Kate Winslet and so on. One such person, who bends spoons and is obviously in touch with some high spirit, came to visit.

David had invited Uri, but was not really expecting him to call, but one evening he arrived unannounced, just like our vicar. What a showman.

We were holding a session at the house and a séance was in progress, this time being held in the green bedroom. I for one was in the garden, as I had been spiritually chased around all evening by the Italian lady. I wanted some peace.

This was not to be. Hearing the car on the drive, I looked up and in they came, bursting through the garden gate, four of them: Uri, his son, a cameraman and a researcher.

Brushing me aside, they entered the house filming everything that moved. Finally, I shouted to David who came and rescued me.

The energy was electrifying - everyone remarked on it - with spoons being bent at ease. Objects and apples floated through the air. Jeff demonstrated how light the gym equipment had become and as for me, well, I put on a show for free.

Yes! It was show time again and the Italian lady gave her best performance. How embarrassing, and I was on camera to! He left as he had arrived: in a swirl of magic and confusion, shouting to David that he would be back soon. We never saw him again, but what a night!

It was not over for us. As this famous person left, grasping at the air and attempting to take the energy with him, his son pleaded with him, saying it would make the dogs at home bark all night.

Immediately I thought of Ben. Where was my Ben? We had not seen him all night. Then someone shouted from the garden.

"Thelma! Come quick and see your dog."

Running out directly, I saw a pitiful sight lying in the shallow pond - breathless and foaming at the mouth, his eyes rolling back into his sockets.

I was panicking and shouting for David. We rang for the vet and that night Ben stayed away from the house and its unforgiving energy.

Our beautiful dog, our friend and companion of 18 years passed away peacefully the following Monday - the 15th of July 1996. We shall never forget him and nor would Jean who had already planned a very special job for him indeed!

The deed is everything the glory nothing.
**Johann Wolfgang von Goethe, Poet, Novelist,
Playwright and Diplomat
(1749-1832)**

Cometh the man with his 'special deed'

To wake them up

To gather them up

Earth bound spirits

To roam no more

To lead them all to safety

Home once more

Through his welcoming starlight, spiritual, open door

Thelma Glanville

CHAPTER 14
FIRE! FIRE!
(Rescue Work Begins - Return of Jean)

The learning process had started. The energy in the house was high and electric. Each Wednesday, we gathered to receive the spirits. The incredible story of our invisible, spiritual guests was unfolding. I channelled many spirits throughout our necessary ordeal. They came with great gusto each time I sat. There was no waiting, especially not for the Italian lady, poor unfortunate soul, still searching for her baby. It was heart breaking.

One by one they came to us: terrified, screaming, confused, crying for their loved ones. Some nights it was too sad to handle. We would cry ourselves, feeling their pain and loss.

A story was being told of a great fire that took place in the year of 1758 at an inn which stood on our very site. Being constructed of wood and tar, it quickly, completely burned down to the ground one autumn night. There was carnage; so many lives were wiped out. A tale of horror and betrayal, guilt and remorse, was being documented.

John P would encourage these poor souls into the light and into thinking they had all gone home to "Mother" - our spiritual home.

Many, many spirits came and went, we all thought! Until one evening Jean returned, our French Egyptian scholar. Whilst on this earth, Jean had studied the pyramids, the constellations and many of earth's other mysteries. He was obsessed with his books; they were his life. Channelling Jean was quite different. A bond had developed which I could not explain. He had spoken through me several times before and had seemed to go into the light. He was a gentle spirit. Quite reserved and well-educated, he'd travelled alone back to his homeland after visiting Bath and Wiltshire, and even as far as York.

I believe that the Egyptian head that appeared on my kitchen wall on the very first night that we received spirit, was his calling card.

The events leading up to the fire were filled with great gaiety. There was a visiting fair in the grounds of the inn with all manner of entertainment. Many spirits relayed this, but I especially remember a rather large lady named Beatrice and a man called Maurice.

Maurice had met his fate in the fire and could remember each detail of his last hours on this earth. Robbed and trussed up by the travellers in the garden, he was thrown into the stables before the fire started. It was heart rending to hear his plight. He was just a traveller who had just stopped for the night - a simple man who the fairground louts had taken advantage of. A young girl named Beth, who was the sister of one of the perpetrators, confirmed this account.

Beatrice was knocked down and trampled underfoot among the chaos.

My heart went out to the Italian lady, as she never found her baby, Mathilda. The baby was left crying and unattended in her room at the inn (our green bedroom) and had no chance of survival. Her mother's guilt was taken to the grave. We offered our love to all these poor souls, especially the children who died in agony on that night.

The inn had been full to capacity, with drinking and merry making and some other dark deeds taking place. A proper lady was staying with her maid Georgina. One of our circle channelled Lady Sumners and I myself channelled Georgina. The antics were just like watching a play:

"Sort it, Georgina," she said, very frustrated. "My hair, my hat is not right, sort it." So demanding. The poor girl never knew which way to turn, until that dreaded night. This chills me even now to recall this wicked deed

Georgina was to get her revenge on her mistress, to her own peril. Collecting the embers from the fire grate for her lady's warming pan, she placed some under the bed to slowly ignite. With great delight she watched her mistress burn.

John P blessed her and prayed that she be forgiven. Finally, he passed them over into the light.

Souls can become trapped on this earthly plane after a violent death

or if they are simply not ready to go. Their lives have been cut short and they are lost and lonely, not fully understanding why they are wandering around. They have failed to go to the loving white light: a circle held in harmony and love to shine a light into the darkness.

We though all were rescued and safely home, until one evening. We were all about to be proven very wrong indeed.

Loud, strong and very forceful, and with a message that shook us all: it was Jean, who had burnt to death that terrible night along with all his fellow beings, yet his message was to lift us all to great heights and expectations.

Recalling his last moments on this earth makes me weep: sitting alone and protecting his precious books and documents, covering his ears to block out their screams; watching the blue smoke curl up through the wooden boards beneath his feet; grasping at his possessions; the thick, choking wood smoke filling his room; the fire now taking hold, crackling and burning - his end very near.

As I channelled Jean, the realisation of being burnt to death was unbearable. As I looked down at my own hands I could see his burning. It took most of the group to convince me that my person was not on fire.

What a way to die. God have mercy on these poor souls. Jean had passed over to paradise, yet returned to this earthly plane to redeem himself.

"Reborn in spirit" - his message, though full of remorse and guilt, was so positive and instructing.

11th September 1996 - Jean channelled by Thelma

All questions asked by John P, David and Dilys after she brings in the energy. (For Jean's light sign and spiritual name, see PAGE VIII for symbols.)

Dilys: *(Crying while John consoles her. Dil bringing energy for Jean to manifest.)*

Thelma (Jean): My name's Jean.

John P: Jean! I thought you'd gone over? *(Gasping at Jean's return)*

Thelma (Jean): Follow me, follow me!

John P: You've come back to help us?

David: Where's your books?

Thelma (Jean): I want to take them out, I WANT TO TAKE THEM OUT. I'VE BEEN REBORN! TO TAKE THEM OUT, I AM HERE, ANYBODY...

David: How can we help?

Thelma (Jean): FOLLOW ME, DON'T CRY.

John P: You can go with Jean to the light. *(Talking to the spirits he was sensing)*

David: How can we help you Jean?

John P: How can we work together?

Thelma (Jean): You can't help me, I am going to do it on my own, I KNOW HOW, THIS TIME I KNOW HOW. I WILL TAKE THEM OUT, I WILL LEAD THEM THIS TIME, I WILL NOT SIT AND BURN AGAIN, I WILL TAKE THEM OUT. I HAVE BEEN REBORN TO DO THIS DEED.

John P: Good Jean, but it is teamwork, we're all willing to help.

Thelma (Jean): NO NOT THIS TIME.

John P: Can we help you?

Thelma (Jean): You rally them together, all of these souls.

David: How can we do that?

Thelma (Jean): RALLY THEM, WAKE THEM UP! TELL THEM THAT I AM BACK, I AM BACK AND I WILL LEAD THEM OUT.

John P: There's no need to shout, remember you're inside! You are welcome and we are glad you've come back. I remember last time when you went. *(A little confused)*

Thelma (Jean): We will lead them.

David: How many souls are there?

Thelma (Jean): Many souls here disgusted, disgusted, but this time my chance, MY CHANCE, MY CHANCE. I will lead them, the poor babies, the poor children, the men, the women.... I sat and did nothing, I SAT AND DID NOTHING. *(Crying)*

John P: That's a lesson Jean. We all have to learn a lesson, you have learned.

Thelma (Jean): I had a sign, a sign to tell you.

David: What was the sign?

Thelma (Jean): A message! You don't understand.

Dilys: Jean, I do understand.

Thelma (Jean): I AM THE LEADER.

John P: Tell us more Jean. We're here to help you!

Dilys: Are the messages within the house?

Thelma (Jean): Many messages, many messages... I was reborn to do this deed.

Dilys: We understand.

Thelma (Jean): MUST I WAIT MUCH LONGER? I WANT TO GATHER THEM UP, ALL UP. NOT MUCH TIME, NOT MUCH MORE TIME. THE DOOR WILL CLOSE!

John P: We will help you.

Thelma (Jean): Damn the books, damn the books, DAMN THE BOOKS!

David: When will the door close?

Thelma (Jean): Soon!

David: When is soon?

Thelma (Jean): Why do you ask me? *(Frustrated)*

Dilys: Listen Jean. We will wake them, we have seen your signs and we are here to help.

Thelma (Jean): So long, so long. *(Speech now distorted. Mentions the* *dates 1758 and 1820)*

John P: So long, that's why we are here, we can all work together. You take them, we will wake them.

David: How can we help? How can we wake them up?

Thelma (Jean): Do not abandon like I did!

John P: We will not abandon you, we are here!

Thelma (Jean): I have gone over, I have come back. I was reborn. *(Very quiet and subdued)*

John P: We were here for you going. *(John thinking he had passed Jean over a week previous - questioning himself)*

Thelma (Jean): I WAS REBORN IN SPIRIT TO HELP, TO FOLLOW, TO LEAD, FOLLOW.

John P: We will waken them, you don't need to shout.

Thelma (Jean): I can hear them, sweet people, sweet souls, sweet spirits. Where are you? Wake up I am here, I want to lead you out this time. *(Now crying)*

John P: They will wake up, we will pray to wake them up. Peace, now, peace. We will pray together

Thelma (Jean): I kept myself to myself, I didn't care about anybody but myself, so I don't know how many people there are. *(Still crying)*

John P: All right, now relax, you are not alone. We helped you to go over and you've come back to help them and us. We all work together that's why we care. It's not one, it's all, and you know this! We will work together and we will wake them up and you may show them the way. This is going to be a great help to you and us.

David: Jean he's gone over? *(Asking John)*

John P: Jean went last time.

David: Did Jean say the year 1758 or 1820? When was he reborn in spirit? *(Confirming that 1758 was the year of the fire and that 62 years later he came back on this earthly plane to plan his Stargate.)*

(A confused discussion follows as to when Jean was reborn in spirit and how he was going to lead the trapped, earth bound spirits out. With the message from Jean now ended the session comes to a close with giving thanks to Jean.)

***

After receiving this message from Jean, events got even stranger. Spirits of all ages and all walks of life were being channelled. Even monks! A young man named Steven, who had been killed in a modern day car crash on the Bath Road in the early 70s, came to us.

Within my husband's quest for knowledge of our site, it came to his notice that any building, in the 18th century without the 'sun sign' was simply not insured and therefore left to its own fate.

Jean highlighted this on the 16th of May 1996, when he left his calling card: the little china sun hanging in the brass pot. Believe me, this was the original place of our doorway before the alterations to the kitchen. How clever of him to give us a clue!

In the year 1758, the sun insurance icon would have been placed over the doorway to represent fire protection. The inn had none. No records could be found of that dreadful night, but what of the dead? Surely one cared. Jean would be their saviour.

Jean had expressed with great grief, that these people of the fire had been burnt on his soul. The joy he must have received on learning he could return to this earth's plane through spirit to lead them home: home to 'Mother' to redeem himself. This he did with a deep longing and desperation, but also with tender love. Jean touched our hearts.

One evening I sat with my husband to give thanks to Jean: a personal message of love from me to him. What a wonderful man, reborn in spirit to lead them out. What courage and determination for a soul who had passed over to paradise and come back to do this deed.

"This time I know how," Jean said, *strong and reassuring.*

Yes! I thought, I also know now, through our spiritual gateway.

It was all making sense now: the lights and explosions in our front garden back in 1987-1988. Jean had punched an opening through to our dimension for a prearranged date and time for our Stargate: the waiting room, the safe place, the gathering in.

On and on we seemed to plunge, deeper and deeper into the depths of human misery, spirit after spirit coming forth with their tales of earthly lives. Like Steven from the car crash, who had simply stated that he'd walked out of the crash, up the Bath Road, and joined the ones waiting in our garden. Yes! Our garden!

We had created a "waiting room for spirits". I even found myself drawing the curtains in each and every room of the house to keep it safe and dark. This was very strange behaviour for me indeed!

A spirit called Matthew talked of the beacon - shining so bright: up, down and around - encouraging the spirits to bathe in this light and to wait for their salvation.

Jean's presence was so strong. He was determined to use our minds and bodies to wake them up, to gather them in: not only the ones from the fire, but every lost soul who wanted to go home.

Through a combination of trance and the psychic link between Dil and me, a special date was emerging when these souls would be passed over. *I used to awake in the morning and immediately have a saying on the tip of my tongue: "Blessed are these who pass this gate." (received 12th Sept 96)*

I would ring Dil and she'd come back saying, "Gather in by the 12th." It felt almost biblical.

Many spirits would confirm that the fire happened in the fall, which we took to be October. This was also confirmed via Dil in a trance.

The night of September 13th 1996, Jeff was alone in the house. Hearing strange noises coming from the gym, he investigated and, to his amazement, found the whole apparatus had been turned around forming some kind of gateway. Sitting on the "pec" seat was

"Watch" in Tabu sign over Gym stopped at 7:15 am. "Stargate Time" Oct 12th 1996 at 7:15 am.

one of David's watches, showing a time of 7.15. He did not know whether it was am or pm, until he discovered that all the other clocks in the house were showing the same time, and our grandfather clock actually showed am.

Had a time been set for our first ever Stargate?

7.15am, 12th October 1996. Everything seemed to point to this date and time. I think Jean gently manipulated Jeff out of the gym for the purpose of the Stargate. It was the passing over or, as John, the gardener, likes to say, the ascension. It was all coming together. A complete pattern had been formed. Yes, we were gathering up as many lost souls as we could in the name of Jean to be passed over to the light through his spiritual gateway on 12th of October 1996, Pentecostal descent of the Holy Spirit to the Apostles, Jewish Harvest, 50 days after pass over, evening of enlightenment.

The spirits, through mind contact, inspired John the gardener to lay out a runway made of large fig leaves, headed with flowers. This ran from the gym window and finished towards the front of the garden, ending up in front of a large Leylandii fir tree with a

"Clock stopped" 7:15 am. "Stargate Time"

top that bent in the most peculiar way. This reminded me of Palm Sunday, when the Jews paved the way for Jesus, their saviour and our King of Kings.

John, the Gardener, had also stated that an alignment of the planets would take place on the 12th: Mars-moon-star-sun, 12th October 1996 at dawn, 7.15am.

The gateway he could see stood eight feet tall, pillars holding up a beautiful archway, flanked with angels to welcome and receive the spirits coming home to Mother. He could see their loved ones waiting on the other side, and my beautiful Ben, sitting patiently at the foot of these pillars, waiting for the children, to encourage them to pass through the spiritual gateway.

I remember Jeff's beautiful message that came to him as a melody one evening:

DO YOU SEE HOW YOUR TREE BENDS DOES IT INSPIRE LEANING OUT TOWARDS YOUR GATEWAY WHERE ALL YOUR KNOWLEDGE IS LEARNT
ARE YOU GETTING SOMETHING OUT OF THIS FOR IT HAS JUST BEGUN
YOU CAN SPEND YOUR TIME ALONE MEDITATE ON YOUR THOUGHTS AND YOU CAN COME TO TERMS AND REALIZE THAT YOU MUST REMEMBER IT MAKES

MUCH MORE SENSE TO LIVE IN THE PRESENT TENSE
BUT DID YOU EVER THINK BEFORE ALL WHAT YOU
NOW KNOW HOW THIS LIFE ENDS
WHEN YOUR ROAD AHEAD COMES TO A DEAD END
FOR YOU WILL TAKE FLIGHT INTO THE AIR INTO A
NEW REALM ASCENDING UP INTO THE LIGHT WITH
ALL YOU HAVE TO TAKE THIS IS YOURS TO KEEP FOR
ETERNITY TO ENTER INTO THE LIBRARY OF THE
STORY OF YOUR LIVES
ALTHOUGH THIS LIFE IS GETTING HARDER TO LIVE
AND CHOICES ARE AT LEAST LITTLE
MAKE OF IT WHAT YOU WILL BUT ALL TIMES
REMEMBER TO LIVE IN YOUR PRESENT TENSE DO NOT
TRY TO ESCAPE REALITY TOO OFTEN

We had one request to Jean: to enter all the names of the souls who would pass through our gateway. We even placed an exercise book on the pec seat of the gym equipment with a pencil at its side.

David of course, to keep his own 'spirits' up, had some fun: communication with Scrabble on our dining room table. He gleaned much information. The pyramids and Sphinx were favourites. They stated that all the answers to all of our 'why's' were under such constructions.

The Sphinx has been adopted by Freemasonry and set outside other sacred buildings. The image symbolizes the guarding of "secret knowledge" within. What is the key for passage or allowed entry?
Alchemy prime numbers can sometimes give you the answers you seek.

DISPLAY OF ALCHEMY PRIME NUMBERS ON SPIRITUAL TABLE. REF:- JOHN P ASKING MALACHI ABOUT THE IMPORTANT OF 'NUMBERS' IN THE SPIRITUAL WORLD. PAGE 81

David liked inviting people into the house who dared to venture to inspect the gym equipment. By this time the spirits, as I stated, had balanced it in the most peculiar way: creating some sort of gateway. What great delight there was in working out how it remained balanced.

David placed some small beer bottles in the gym for them to play with. The spirits would oblige him by balancing the apparatus on top of these bottles, forming funny little groups on the floor and laying them out in strange ways to form symbols or some kind of weird writing.

Until one day, the fun stopped! Arriving home one evening, we found to our amazement that both the doors to the gym had been sealed. Yes! Firmly shut. By what force we have no idea. There were no locks or keys for the doors and even when pressure was applied they would not budge. Taboo signs had been hung over the doorways. A clear statement to all: "KEEP OUT NO ENTRY".

Placed carefully in the open mouth of one of the signs were a large, wooden, African head and a wristwatch confirming the time of the opening of the spiritual gate.

We ran upstairs to check the void in Nick's bedroom, which is directly above the gym and which we also suspected would be used for their purpose. It was still open! Hesitantly we looked in, not knowing what to expect. Before us, lay an incredible sight. All the area was swept clean. A runway had been spiritually prepared using some of the artefacts from the void. Jean had given us privileged time to inspect his preparations for the Stargate.

Not long after this date, this entrance was also closed by the spirits and similar taboo signs were placed over the doorway.

You should be aware that most paranormal events happen very fast; a twinkling of an eyelid and changes are made.

Symbolic Sign. Nick's void (bedroom) showing a runway for Stargate 12/10/1996. Normally full to the brim of toys now all gone cleared.

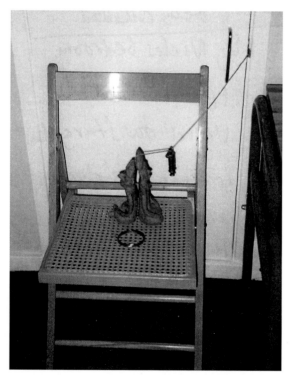

Nick's bedroom void now sealed looking like an Egyptian Tomb with seals - Jean's work

Beyond the veil

Wisdom is stored

Wisely given to the 'chosen one'

Within the accordance of spiritual law

Thelma Glanville

CHAPTER 15
GREAT TEACHING

September 20th 1996 was a night of great excitement. It started as a sociable evening, with good friends calling round for an update on our spooks. Jeff was there that evening and things were as normal as they could be in our house! Drinks were flowing and a lovely atmosphere was felt by all. This was a real treat for me. Trying to keep everybody in my sight that evening was a hard task as I was really enjoying the pleasures that real friendship can bring.

Full of curiosity, my friend's daughter slipped away unnoticed. I did not welcome investigation of the house, as things were developing in such a way that I had become very protective.

There are two doors to the gym: one from the den and one from the kitchen.

"Does this door open to the gym?" she shouted through from the kitchen, leaning on the door with all her might, trying her hardest to open it.

Without any indication and no warning at all, up jumped a very furious Jean, channelled through me in a semi-trance. Voice raised, he commanded that "all unbelievers must leave and leave now!"

Embarrassed and confused, her parents took their leave almost immediately, as Jean made no bones in his demands, but in fact stood over them, pointing the way out! Reprimanding their daughter and quite upset, they disappeared through the door. I had no control over such events. I did not want my friends to leave, but Jean was out to protect the sealed area at all costs!

With the sudden entrance of Jean the evening took on a whole different meaning. The events that followed took us all completely by surprise and left us in wonderment.

Jeff. Yes, Jeff, our reluctant hero, manifested into a semi, eye-staring trance. In a very calm and controlled voice, he channelled the following, occasionally interrupted by a noisy Jean. Words of enlightenment and great teaching were about to told, with a few surprises for us all, about to be told...

**

20th 1996 September - Jeff in trance (adapted by Roy Dutton, March 1997).

Interpretation of the taped extract of the in-trance message published in Contact International's 'Awareness' magazine, Volume 21 Number 4, Spring 1997.

By T.R. Dutton

Introduction

A taped extract of a much longer message given by a person in trance was published recently in the 'Awareness' magazine of the UFO Research group, Contact International. The message was one element of a series of strange events, which have beset a family in Reading, Berkshire, over a period of months. The happenings appear to be UFO related, but there seems also to be strong elements of spiritualism and religion. Data Research, who transcribed the message, commented on this; and noted the sometimes-garbled nature of the message. A request for the assistance of readers in the process of interpretation was issued. This is my response to that request.

The Nature of the Message

It is not unusual for messages received in trances to become garbled at times; but this can be regarded as evidence that the prophet or medium is not exercising discernment during the trance, and that the conscious mind has become temporarily disengaged.

Although grey aliens from elsewhere in the universe are referred to, the theme of the message is very similar to that found in the apocalyptic writings of the Hebrew prophets. The message seems to be a 'last days' warning.

The reference to the 'Sun…. which Malaki knew' is very intriguing, because the last book of the Old Testament of the Bible happens to be Malachi (pronounced Malaki). Furthermore, in chapter four, verse two, we find a prophecy, which states that, the 'Sun of righteousness' shall arise 'with healing in his wings'. Scholars believe that this imagery originated as the winged disc of the Sun God, which often appeared in Persian and Egyptian religious art of that period (430 to 460BC). This seems to link very well with the reference made, during the trance, to the ancient Egyptians.

The message seems to imply that souls have been repeatedly reincarnated throughout the Ages and that in these 'Last Days' many will cease to exist, because they have allowed themselves to die in this life, by following entirely materialistic creeds. So, here again, we have a recognisable link established with Biblical Prophecy—that Apocryphal book, the second book of Esdras (Fourth book of Ezra in the Catholic Bible) springing immediately to mind.

[I read somewhere that the number of people living today is the same as the total of all people who have ever lived throughout Man's existence on this planet. So, in terms of reincarnated souls (if one can accept such a concept) massive losses at this proclaimed critical time in history could be seen as being a major catastrophe with eternal consequences.]

My progressive interpretation of the literal message now follows. So far, I have been unable to find any reference to 'arages' and 'adgerate' (or to words with similar pronunciation) in any of my reference books, so I have allowed the context to suggest their interpretations whenever they occur.

The Interpreted Message (to be cross-referenced with the original):

The aliens and their world are dying.
Who the little greys [or graylings] are, is irrelevant.
Their arages [souls] are similar to ours but have a different form.
They have different ways of life and different needs.
All our souls have lived for countless aeons.
This life is not all we know.
This life is not the end - it's just part of the journey.
When we leave it we take knowledge of it with us and take on other forms within the Universe. This process will go on eternally.
This is the End [last days of the Earth?]. We are living at the End. The little aliens have lived [existed] for many thousands of years. Now they are dying out and don't know why. They believed themselves to be immortal but now they are dying and their souls are returning to the Mother [God, the Universe].
We humans have forgotten how to move on when we die. Think of the Pyramids. The Egyptians knew all about this and also had very advanced technology. It's all been lost.
That's why Jean has been chosen to come back from the afterlife - to help the people that are here. An advanced way of life has been lost. There are a few people still alive who understand but who will not share their knowledge.
The [truth] is coming out, but not quickly enough. There are too many people and many will be lost during this life because they don't understand and believe. They've lost their souls.
This is a chance for people "to join the Mother" [rediscover their souls?]. You are simple life form [like an amoeba] and you know so little compared with what you will know - when you pass from here and experience "there". We will not have human bodies. People forget [past-life experiences?]. I don't know why. The Sun of Malachi has

something [work?] to do.

Something is taking the adgerate[past-life memory?]. That's why life must end. It's being taken away by [academic concepts of life]. The adjuras is part of the universal system of life and therefore cannot be destroyed, but a [localised] counterforce is building up against it.

The Mother is known to us as God - all unbelievers must leave [the séance room?]!

Whatever is endangering the adjuras is not interested in knowledge but is interested only in energy [power]. It's building up an alternative power structure. In the final battle between good and evil [Armageddon] people can overrule evil. The destructive alternative system will be destroyed.

People who have no beliefs can't pass over [when they die?] - This is why we call it evil.

These people will be those who chose an alternative [power] structure, which are drawing as many as possible to gain more power. This [atheistic] structure cannot shut down the whole system of life, but there is another system on this side [in the spirit-world?], which can. What we know as evil is not personal. It is not a personal devil. It is not what we are doing to the planet. There's a body of people on this planet that have known it [the real evil?] for a long time.

Since the time of the [ancient] Egyptians there has been a [spiritual?] downfall of people."

The closing lines of the extracted message seemed to be questions asked subconsciously by the medium, followed by the answers received:

The Egyptians had come up [been mentioned]. Everything seems to have been so advanced up to and including the time of the Aztecs [and, possibly, the Incas?].

I am fascinated for [by] the aliens and asking about them. I am getting [being told] that the aliens had come to this earth for our help and we had not given it.

We don't want to give it. We want their technology. We want their everlasting total [fulfilled?] life.

We want their secret life. We want their technology. We are so selfish.

They are not evil. [It's not a matter of good and evil]. They have not the same [concepts?].

Footnote
T.R.Dutton

If we can relate to the world-view being presented, it becomes evident that whoever is responsible for the messages is deeply concerned for the human souls. The extraterrestrial aliens are being portrayed as just examples of a different form of psychical life which has its own problems, the main one being the physical death of the species.

In contrast, we are being told that the human problem is of a magnitude which is doubly catastrophic, because it involves the imminent death of our planet with all its species of life, coupled with a man-made interruption of the universal process of soul migration. We are being told that if this disruptive process is allowed to continue, human souls will be destroyed, en masse, with the planet.

Of course, this concern for souls is very much at the heart of most of the world's leading religions-especially, Christianity. Take these words of Jesus for example: '...Fear not them, which kill the body, but are not able to kill the soul: but rather fear him which is able to kill both soul and body in hell.'

So that part of the Christian message is basically the same, in essence, as the message being transmitted through the young man in Reading. The reference to "the Sun of Malachi" ["with healing in his wings"] also points us towards the need for spiritual healing. Biblically, this "Sun" is related to the promised new Elijah, interpreted by Christians as being John the Baptist, who prepared the way for Jesus.

We are being informed that the little grey aliens need our help, but that it is not yet forthcoming. According to Jesus, the way to save one's soul is by learning how to relate to God and, unselfishly, to others. Since, today, many of us find it difficult to meet these requirements in our complex and materialistic human society, an unselfish response to the poor little aliens' [Flying Dutchman's] plight might provide a necessary stimulus to prepare us for the day when, we are told, all we humans shall [very suddenly] be launched into eternity.

For me this has been a very thought-provoking exercise, which I can only hope has had similar effects on others. My thanks go to all concerned - to the family in Reading and to members of Contact International for being sufficiently uninhibited, by the strange nature of the message, to publish it for the potential benefit of all. It most certainly adds a new twist to the UFO enigma!

END
T.R.Dutton

***

Also that night, we received all manner of confirmations:

The utmost importance of crop circles - one day in our earthly calendar, a great spiritual teacher will be given the answer to their meaning on this earth. Crop circles appeared in our deep pile rugs, with a carefully placed everyday Yale key directly beneath the beautiful patterns - a key left to open up the door to these mysteries to our future on this earth, the unsolved mysteries that hold people captive. What were they trying to tell us?

The scroll containing a photograph of Tutankhamun appeared on the table to us in a twinkle of an eye, like an Egyptian scroll of life trying to convey us all the secrets of the ancient world. It was beautifully presented, held firmly together with one of my own dress rings.

UFOs, Little Grey Aliens, the Great Universe - the last of the great unknown - all life's mysteries that we humans are always questioning. Searching out the truth, spending most of our earthly lives on this never-ending quest just like our sweet Jean.

On nights like these we were in awe of the spirits and wondered, "Why us? Why have we been chosen?" It was becoming an honour.

The Book of Malachi

The last of the twelve Old Testament books which bear the names of the Minor Prophets, grouped together as "The Twelve" in the Jewish canon. The author is unknown: Malachi is merely a translation of a Hebrew word meaning "my messenger". The prophet defends the justice of God to a community that had begun to doubt that justice because its eschatological (end of the world) expectations were still unfulfilled.

Ref to transcript of T.R.Dutton

CHAPTER 16
CHANGE OF DIRECTION

Spirits came thick and fast once again. I felt their touches, like invisible hands caressing me tenderly and lovingly, feeling me through another dimension like cobwebs gently falling, keeping me close at hand.

Some diversity was required so John P and Gina suggested holding some meetings at their home. Gina is such a great host and this was most welcomed.

A spirit manifested itself to me in trance, naming himself Malachi. He was a strong, powerful man - a Sun God. He filled me up with his presence until I had doubled my size.

With a powerful voice, he boomed out messages on many subjects, talking to the group as though they were his children.

"You are sitting to my side, sit in front of me my children," he bellowed.

Again and again he would demand respect and took great delight in repeating and giving the meanings to all of our names.

We took heed of his warnings and messages, after all, his name is mentioned in the bible. He stayed with the group for many months to come, and sometimes he could be quite entertaining, although a bit arrogant. The second time he manifested, David asked him a question.

He gave no answer, but just replied, "Ha. I do believe you are the vessel's *beloved*," rolled his head and gave out a great roaring laugh.

This thoroughly amused David and 'beloved' stuck to him throughout.

John P would ask about the importance of numbers within the spiritual realm and ask about their meanings, referring to the ancient world of alchemy. These questions he would not answer, too rude when ladies were present. Little did we know that Malachi's days were numbered for reasons that would soon become apparent to us.

John P's teaching included spiritual healing - the art of meditation for our inner peace. He introduced us to many books and videos and opened up another world to us all. This, I think, helped David to fully come to terms with the great intrusion into our lives.

John P even took us to London to meet Sirius, a Brazilian lady who had experienced some very strange encounters indeed - I mean of the third kind! This I found very hard to handle at first, but the more I listened, the more I came to terms with this concept, not knowing that this would be part of my fate later on in my ordeal. I have great respect for her, for she had taken this on board and her lifestyle had changed dramatically in so many ways. Her husband had left her and no support was being offered from her family - she was an outcast for what she believed in. Who was I to sit in judgement when my own life seemed to be in real turmoil.

At this meeting we met two spiritual ladies who performed regressions for people's past lives to help with their karmas. They had been observing me very closely and, of course, John P had already told them of our spiritual events at home. They asked if they could visit the house with a hopeful tone.

At that time I was quite stressed about being away from home, as I felt I should be standing on guard, but we finally agreed that they could visit, as they had great understanding of our situation.

Finally, the day came. They inspected the house with respect, but with the usual curiosity. They both came across the void in Nick's bedroom.

By this time there was a very odd spiritual display placed neatly on a chair, barricading the door, along with taboo signs similar to those in the gym. To my horror, one of the ladies tried to open the door, which then came ajar allowing her to peep in.

With great concern, once again I went into one of my rages shouting at her to leave it alone! Fearing the worst, I slammed the door shut. Very polite and unruffled, she simply said sorry and asked if I could ask my spirit guide if all was well.

This we had done many times, as David's friends always seemed to knock over the displays left around the house. Sitting them in the dining room, my favourite place for trance, I asked Jean to correct the breach and he confirmed that all was well.

All the time, the two ladies and David were sitting by my side. I came out of trance in the normal way. Almost at once I felt something strange enter my head and then I saw a large shape like a bubble surround me. No! I was not imagining this; I could see it quite clearly. I have received spirit in so many strange ways since I became psychic, but this was quite different. This was telepathic. Yes! Someone was just talking to me and simply giving me a message of thanks for the help that we were giving for the forthcoming Stargate and saying how much it was appreciated.

It was not allowed to answer any questions, put by the two ladies, other than to say that it was from the fifth dimension. It simply disappeared as it had come, in its own bubble - its form of transport. Although it left me a bit confused, calmness filled me like I had been with this being before.

I was completely overwhelmed with the feeling of peace and love for this creature.

We are all beings of light, creations of Mother/God.

***

I would like to take a moment to remember a poor unfortunate soul who lived a lonely life and experienced poverty and the cruelty of his fellow man - an outcast of the human race - simply, a tramp.

Lunchtime - a welcome break from the office. Jeff and I snuck out for a quick bite and a natter with our friends at the tea-rooms in Caversham, a small village on the outskirts of Reading. To arrive at our destination, we had to drive under two old railway bridges along the road which runs parallel to the River Thames - one of Reading's beauty spots. Our lunchtime also included rushing to the bank and a quick look around the shops. The earlier we went to lunch the better, as the traffic built up later in the afternoons.

I remember this event quite clearly. It was a bright sunny day when we drove to the bank via this route, and the traffic was light, so Jeff was enjoying the drive. Emerging from under the bridge into the sunlight, all was well with the world. Until we were greeted by an awful grinding noise coming from the gear stick. Looking at each other, we laughed.

"Oops. Sounds like a garage job to me," I said, still laughing.

"No! There is nothing wrong with my car," answered Jeff quite crossly.

"All right, can't you take a joke?" I said looking out of the window and wondering to myself what this dreadful noise could have been.

Jeff is very proud of his company car and keeps it in tiptop condition. Every single noise gets immediate attention.

Lunchtime was over and it was time to return to work. Driving back via the same route, sure enough, just before the bridge, we heard the same awful noise. This time it was much louder and made the gear stick vibrate. Slowing down, we hoped it would cease, but it grew in its anger and finally threw Jeff's hand off, quite violently.

"Did you see that," he yelled.

"Not only did I see it, I felt it," I said, now very excited.

The spiritual energy that passed through the car was electrifying. This was wonderful. Yet there were no thoughts or hints of who or what it was. Perhaps someone had been in an accident on this very spot and had not passed over.

This event happened several more times on this journey, until one day the energy was so strong and demanding the spirit completely filled me.

"Don't be frightened. I know you are here."

I spoke tenderly and with compassion, for I felt the deep longing for contact. This I have felt many times before, especially the very first time with beautiful Jean.

"Please, please stay with us, we will take you home, a place of safety, trust us." Tears fell as I spoke. The noises coming from the gear stick were terrific.

"Jeff, drive home now. No time to wait," I said urgently.

There was not minute to lose; the spirit was so strong and the trance was now manifesting. As we pulled into the drive, I jumped out of the car.

"Slow down, I can't walk that fast."

The spirit had finally spoken. Immediately, my body seemed to take on an old man's form. My back now bent, I slowly walked into the house, helped by Jeff. These feelings of "taking on" the form and facial expressions of the person in spirit, are something I have experienced before.

As I entered the house, an awful feeling came over me. He spoke to me once again:

"I am not used to being indoors."

Jeff helped me into the den and sat me down on a small low stool. As I crouched down, holding my body, full trance emerged. I became a man called Lenny and we recorded his last memories on this earth.

Offering our love and protection, we asked him to stay and bathe in the light and safely gathered him in for Jean's special day. *Lenny was a well know tramp who had lived most of his life on the road, and in later years, had made his home under one of the railway bridges at Cow Lane. His domain consisted of cardboard and newspaper covered with some old plastic sheeting.*

He suffered a heart attack and had a spell in hospital, but finally returned only to be abused by three youths who set him on fire, from which he never recovered.

God bless you Lenny.

CHAPTER 17
TIME TO GO PUBLIC

After my encounter with the telepathic being, ET the question was: "What now? How do we proceed?"

Reading an article in one of John P's magazines, we found that a meeting was being held at Kidlington near Oxford regarding UFOs and the Paranormal. David and I decided to attend.

We met all sorts of people from all walks of life, some with similar problems to ours. It was a great feeling to be able to open up and talk about all our fears to people who understood and, above all, wanted to listen.

We spoke to an Oxford professor about our forthcoming event, not really thinking that it would stay in his mind. He informed a production team from *The Why Files*. The information given resulted in a half-hour video for cable television, which I recall in detail. It was harrowing experience to let such people walk all over the house, especially our "special room".

After this meeting, so many interesting people visited the house. A man with dowsing rods confirmed that we had treble ley lines running through the house from the front garden to the rear, straight through our dining room! (Ley lines are earth's own energy fields). David was taught how to use these divining rods and found a new purpose to enhance his spiritual path.

During our spiritual ordeal, we wrote to so many people for help, all to no avail. Then we met Ernie at the Oxford meeting. He was very spiritual and confirmed that extra terrestrials were connected to the spiritual realm. This was music to my ears.

I needed to know more about my visitor in the bubble and how it fitted into our lives at this stage of our spiritual pathway. I was still the curious person that liked to solve mysteries.

Ernie's personal letter to me after our meeting at Kidlington and phone call.

Thursday 3rd October 1996

Dear Thelma,

What an interesting chat we had last night on the phone, you certainly do seem to be in a strange situation up there at your home and I hope the 12th October proves something or the other, I don't know what at present!

Things certainly ARE moving much faster now with reference to the world situation, although our political "masters" are shrugging it all on one side, hoping that it will all blow over. I must admit I sometimes think that the "aliens", as we call them, will finish what they are here to do, maybe producing those hybrid entities for their own planetary system, and leave us to it, since we seem to be self destructive as a species... However, no one really KNOWS.

I'd love to be able to come to your place and personally experience whatever it is about that sealed room. Strangely enough, although maybe NOT, my lady friend from Somerset is coming up here for the weekend on Thursday the 10th October so if anything dramatic happens we will at least be together! She is not into the same things as I am but treats it all with an open mind, however she has SEEN the healing she gets change her life for the better in the last two years or so, and listens to my anecdotes with interest. We are mostly on the same level with our interests in dancing and country music, jazz, etc, plus walking in the countryside which is nice. Her son Jonathan however is really keen on the "paranormal", especially UFO's and such.

I am enclosing some cuttings which may fit in with your interest in the connections twixt "aliens" and the spiritual side... Psychic News and /or the Psychic World would probably be instructive and even "educational"... you can get Psychic News at your local paper shop on order or even in the bigger ones off the shelf weekly, on Thursdays, while Psychic World is a monthly one on subscription... if you need any help on that try me.

I have been involved with the paranormal since an out of body experience when I was just nine years old! In 1933! No doubt that it really happened although my mother didn't like the idea.

Not a lot happened after that until 1960 with that UFO pursuit I spoke about at Oxford... then it all went on from there, fourteen sightings, a "cosmic consciousness" experience during the last sighting in 1978 followed by what seemed to be poltergeistic or even religious incidents until I had the gift of healing dropped into my lap in 1979 when I went into a trance at a healing session. Subsequently I became mediumistic etc. Currently it still happens spontaneously, so my guide Lui Chang some six or seven years ago after I'd been told about him by various mediums over the years... he intends to look after my personal life with advice, relationships, even the sexual side etc, etc, and the apparent "alien" source have made themselves known in the last year or two, complete with abductions, I believe, although I now recognise that those childhood and thence adult poltergeistic and "religious" incidents etc were really "contacts" with them.

Many goes on here in "bursts" of peculiar incidents, it is fairly quiet at the moment! Conscious that I can "step over" into another dimension at times to interact with whatever is there. As they have done with me at odd times a "being" I encountered here in my lounge last year who vanished as he swung around to face me was repeated with a close friend of mine the same evening at his home, before I had even told him about mine.

Perhaps the enclosed cutting will explain better Thelma!

I have been trying to write my book for some years but my viewpoint has changed so much as to what I believe about UFO's etc that it has been revised twice and now needs a drastic complete rewrite... A boring task but one I must get done too, although writing "THE END" will be the most difficult part, I have the most strong goose pimples as I wrote that bit.... A sure sign that there is a "presence" around... quite often my first wife who died in 1947 of tuberculosis, but who appeared in a sun-lit garden, looking absolutely beautiful and healthy, in 1982, speaking a few meaningful words to me before vanishing... she is never far away, more so when I am healing and need extra help. Others have seen her recently as I heal but I am just "aware" of her.

You can maybe see that the book will have to be written before long!

I will close on that note, Thelma. Perhaps you will write back or communicate with me on what is happening or has happened. How do you feel about the so called "coincidences"?

Which ARE NOT, mostly.

I have been asked to do an article on that by Psychic News, only last week - will keep you informed on that. Even meeting YOU at Oxford might well have been such, it is one of the many intriguing aspects of all this, people come into one's lives for a REASON. I have had a spate of such lately, even people I THOUGHT I'd know for years have suddenly broached the subject of UFO'S etc as their deep interest.

Best wishes anyway,
ERNIE

★★★★

The big dilemma of whether to talk to the media about the spiritual experiences that have changed all our lives forever had to be thought about very carefully.

The question is always "what do they believe?" The fact that it is ongoing and that we are now in the advance learning stages of our spiritual journey always brings me back to reality and I thank God for this. It's all true.

The producer of *The Why Files,* a paranormal programme dealing with all kinds of weird subjects, asked us as a group if we would like to make a ten minute programme to fit in with other stories.

It seemed that the professor David and I had met at the UFO meeting at Kidlington had done his job very well, informing on us. At first, we were not really very happy about talking to such people, as we were on our guard. I for one had not even heard of the programme, so as a group we discussed the matter and decided not to go ahead.

But the phone calls never stopped. They suggested that we should meet and have a quiet talk, reassuring us that the programme would be in the "best possible taste" as comedian, Kenny Everett, would say. After some further persuasion, we decided to meet the man in charge, who turned out to be a clairvoyant. This was wonderful and such a relief. In fact he had already obtained much information about our group and he knew all about the events leading up to our Stargate.

The team had arranged to meet us all at my home one evening at about 6.00pm We were told it would only take a couple of hours and then they would be gone, which was fine by us.

Our group gathered in the early afternoon, still not sure whether this was the right thing to do.

6.00pm arrived and in they came: a crew of six armed with cameras, lights, leads, plug sockets, boxes, books, clipboards, grips full of all sorts. My house was soon taken over and looked like Steptoe's yard. We were overwhelmed. "A quiet talk" indeed; the making of the programme was to go ahead that very night!

Alan, the clairvoyant, was very charming and so relaxed; it made it more acceptable to us all. One video was produced. How successful? We shall wait and see.

From the galaxy they came

To give us warnings, guidance and love

Speak not with tongue

But in thine mind

To remind us all, so little time

To bring all our earthy nations into line

Thelma Glanville

CHAPTER 18
ENLIGHTENMENT FROM OUR
DIMENSIONAL FRIENDS

My thoughts were quite clear: it was not a spirit but an extra terrestrial that visited me on that day of the breach. When it came in its own protective bubble. This feeling became so strong within me. I spoke to many ET's after this event telepathically.

They reminded me of a simple but urgent message that I had been told before, but where and how?

"The human race must learn to live in harmony with his neighbour. Stop destroying this earth before it's too late or suffer the consequences. The question is not shall the earth survive but the human race itself? We have become too dangerous for our own good. We must change spiritual and morally. The dimensional shift is in progress and time is short."

Our dimensional friends are watching the earth and its inhabitants very closely. These extra terrestrial light beings have our best interests at heart. They are trying very hard to teach us the spiritual knowledge which has been lost to us, to raise our vibrations and to take us out of the mire. The question hangs over the survival of the human race. They have tried many times to communicate with the proper authorities, much to their peril. The special technology they have given us over the last 50 years has now been put on hold. We have misused it for our own greed and not for the benefit of the poor people. A different kind of knowledge may be given, which can be controlled through a wise spiritual leadership, yet to be chosen.

Each time I received these "beings", I seemed to develop an ear problem. The condition seemed to favour the night, flaring up without warning and then just going for no apparent reason. I spoke to my sister Dil about this and, to my amazement, she started to develop the same problem. Discussing certain subjects, somebody would always "tune in" and our ear problem would return.

The burning sensation and ringing was similar to tinnitus. It would travel to the back of the ear to the neck region. This was unexplained and very strange as we both felt it was not a medical problem.

Jeff also complained of a small lump that appeared from time to time at the nape of the neck, which when touched would give out a small electric shock.

But what the heck! Our lives were becoming stranger as time progressed; but more questions needed to be answered, realisation had set in just how really close us three were becoming, but why?

The issue of the ETs was not going to go away. The question of abductions would have to be answered, but were we ready for such revelations? Regression was suggested for a later date, but at this moment in time, there was rescue work to be done.

The big question is when and how we connected with ET's - yet another chapter in our lives to be solved.

CHAPTER 19
ONE DARK AND RAINY NIGHT

We had many nights of laughter and hysterics. One night Jeff and I were at home alone. Hearing the rain lashing against the windowpanes we sat snugly in our den, with dinner trays on our laps, watching one of Jeff's videos. We were thoroughly enjoying the evening and for a fleeting moment, we forgot about our invisible friends.

The rain had set in early that day and had not improved all evening. The night had become dark and murky and yes - things started to happen. Hearing a strange noise from the direction of the stairs, I went to investigate only to find that the statue of the monk, which stood on the twist of the stairs, had gone - just vanished!

"Jeff. The spirits are preparing a surprise for us. Mr Tuck is gone," I informed him.

Rejoining him in the den I tried to settle, but felt very apprehensive. Jeff of course carried on eating and drinking, as these things were now the norm in our house. An hour passed by and, after being lured back into the video, we were totally relaxed.

Beside Jeff's chair stands a gold leaf stand, which he places his drink on. This action is always done without lifting his head and without taking his eyes off the TV, but this night was different. He tried to place his cup as normal only to feel the air.

"Bloody hell. The stand is gone. They've taken it from under our noses. When did they do that?" he spluttered. "Look they've left the little ashtray on the carpet marking the spot.

Obviously that wasn't needed," he added, laughing his head off.

"What have you done with my stuff?" I shouted.

I ran through the house, searching followed by Jeff. We both saw the funny side of the situation. Suddenly, a loud knock at the front door rang through the house. We looked at each other and stood there in silence.

"Are they knocking at the door now?" I whispered.

No visitors ever came to our front door. Opening it sheepishly, we both peered out into the darkness. There, standing in the porch-way, was my friend's daughter and her boyfriend.

"What?" she said.

We must have frightened her with our searching eyes.

"Oh what a relief. It's only you," I said.

She must have thought we were mad, as I pushed past her, closely followed by Jeff, and ran out into the wet and windy front garden. This was the only place we had not looked.

"Jesus, it's out here Jeff," I shouted frantically, "Come and look at this sight."

I was now full of excitement. The rain was pouring down on my gold leaf stand which was standing in the flowerbed outside the gym room window with the monk balancing on top. What a sight for the postman and the passengers on the No 9 bus.

The night the gold leaf stand was taken, leaving the ash tray on the carpet.
The stand was put into the front garden with my "Monk" placed on top.

To protect it from the weather, and our blushes, we covered it up with a large black polythene bag. There it stood until the day of the Stargate. A symbolic gesture for us and the souls - a sign of deliverance - how beautiful and comforting. I don't remember what happened to our guests that night.

A symbolic gesture for us and the souls

Darkness falls, when we are having pleasure

Comes to steal our precious treasure

Collected in love

Stolen in hate and greed

But help is on hand

For the special one who wants to lead

Thelma Glanville

CHAPTER 20
THIEF IN THE NIGHT

Night of Thursday 10th Oct 1996. Every spirit has balance, but not Bhalore. Bhalore is purely negative.

Through mediation and trance Jeff learned that Bhalore is a name for Satan /eternal darkness/negativity.

Our normal place for eating and relaxing was the den, and this night was no different from any other night in our house. We were trying very hard to be a normal, everyday family. I had already eaten and David's dinner was being kept warm in the oven, as he had not yet arrived home, but Jeff was still tucking in and my Nick had already left and gone to his nan's.

Having realised how strange our lives have become, I sometimes shout out to the world to clear my head. Shouting out your thoughts is sometimes therapeutic if done in a positive way. This night I wanted to shout!

"We are mad just sitting here next to a sealed room filled to the brim with spirits, waiting to be beamed up," I shouted out, giving myself a good laugh. "How is anybody going to believe us?" Still joking.

"Mum, give it a rest," came the remark from Jeff.

"Well Jeff. What is it all about?" I paused before continuing. "We never invited this into our home. Why us?"

I was again looking for answers.

"Mum, you look tired. Don't worry. I have a feeling that we are well protected and what we are doing is right," he said, reassuring me.

Well! Such revelations from my son! We had all been through so much in the past six months, sometimes things did not seem real and yes, I was tired.

I returned to the kitchen and carried on chatting to Jeff as he was still in earshot. Staring out of the window into the garden my thoughts started to float and my head became very light. My whole being seemed to be entering another dimension.

I was brought out of this daze-like state quite instantaneously. Jeff was in trouble. He was choking and coughing. His face had turned blue. Throwing the tray on the floor, I thumped his back with fury, now fully aware of the serious situation that he was in. To my amazement, Jeff was trying desperately to speak whilst pointing towards the gym door. To my horror it, I saw it was ajar. Whatever was coming from this room was bombarding my son, filling the air with a taste of acid. Jeff was in real pain. Swinging around, I swiftly closed the door and held it with all my strength. Thank God David came through the door at precisely that moment.

2nd door to gym via the den, now shut after breach from the attempt to steal souls.

With an accusing voice David shouted, "Who opened that bloody door, what were you thinking about?" not even giving us time to explain. I had never seen him so upset!

When David had finished securing the door it looked like Fort Knox. The door securely tied up, poor Jeff recovered. After we explained to David what had happened, he felt very guilty for shouting and gave me a reassuring cuddle. It was a stressful time for all of us, but as a family we had to cope to get through this necessary ordeal, as a lot was at stake.

Jeff was correct we did have someone protecting us, but why did this door open and who opened it? All would be revealed to us.

The gym had been the first place where we had felt the presence of the monks who are buried in the garden. Spiritual evidence of a monastery and graves were found by a medium from London who visited our home on Sunday 6th October 1996 - just before our Stargate. He could see them walking or floating in and around the trees. Also he had other revelations for us all!

We produced a written account of his findings, spoken in trance, as he wandered around the house and gardens:

THE CAVALIER

Named Joseph (Deremont/Dermount or Drew)

Age 35. Date 1642.

Wife Anna nee Fuller. Also daughter. Virtuous man, intelligent. Man of the King, who was butchered for fun by violent men from the North who were unintelligent. Joseph has a cordial rank and says "great evil" will come to the county if the King is killed "let that be a warning".

He now calms down and speaks to us through the medium. He is small and has a large hat and was here between 300 to 400 years ago. He was close to the King but was a landowner. The medium sees a map in the museum of the shires carved up. He was a local man. The Boswell Battle has been mentioned in which he served - also Oakleigh near

Newbury, Berks where there was another battle. We now hear his accent which is Welsh. He is educated and spiritual in mind, his emotions are powerful. He says don't trust servants, they are traitors. He says, "God save the King".

He was taken into a locked room in the inn. Tortured by sword and castrated and was then burnt in a fire which nobody came and put out. His wife and child also died. The inn name which came through is (The Ten Bells) (The Wheat Sheaf) (The Sun and Moon).

Artillery found here on site were Spanish Muskets, small cannon balls and pieces of sword and a grass scythe (pieces of). The drinking was kept quiet here as they were Puritans. On his horse was a blanket and wooden saddle and his sword was held up in front of his face. There were a lot of banners being waved as they faced battle and lot of noise.

There was a sense of humour and the pay he says was low. He was with the 1st or 4th Royal Dragoons.

All kept quiet about his death. No information was recorded by quill. No one will name traitors. No one can trust no one or anyone left. Everybody shopped everyone. Please help me.

Hurrying things up, he would rather keep it for a few months. Several phases of energy, opening an inner dimension, weekly taking them back to the vortex.

THE HALL WAY

Could see a man hanging from a tree - rough justice - an innocent man.

THE GYM *(Did not enter room as door closed by spirits)*

Lots of energies and pulsations. Don't touch, but you are welcome, medium here you have been fooled, but you will never get to the bottom of this. Come in the name of Jesus, come to deliver this soul. He is a monk. More power coming through. All the monks inside are singing.

"We're all monks and we have gone astray". On the outside of the gym is a drainpipe which was an altar. The power is very strong in this area.

THE GREEN ROOM

Here is a little Victorian girl in bright clothing. She has been here many years. She has run away from an orphanage, which was run by a vicar. He was paid well for this but did not look after the children. She died of hunger. The date given - 1860. She is very frightened and very lovely.

THE VOID *(Did not enter void as door closed by spirits)*

Here is the lovely Sister of Mercy in a time warp working for the gentleness of Christ. This is a gradual thing of time and brings mercy and blessings to you all, upon you all. Lots of meditation. Good hands, guiding, knowledge. Penetrate further into their laws. Please no harm.

OUTSIDE

Artesian well 50ft deep - (marked the spot). Large brown dog. Buried goats and pigs around. A cattle market nearby.

Temple of Minerva. Romans had statue of Venus in the garden, columns were a roman villa belonging to a Governor. Grapes growing, herbs also growing. People from afar visited, even Africa. Lots of magic and learning going on in these times.

Monks built here within the ruins. Also about 24 graves from the monastery in the garden. Monks can be seen walking through.

This strange and revealing account of our house and garden was recorded by one of our group members.

UFO over house night before Stargate
11th Oct 1996 - approx 7:30pm

Very bright small light, 2-3 seconds, silent. Left a white light trail 5-10 seconds after.

3-4,000 feet, low? Not a shooting star.

Went over trees and disappeared.

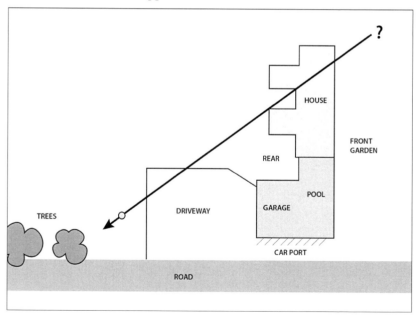

CHAPTER 21
A HEAVENLY SIGN IN THE SKY

Reply from the Ministry of Defence to our letter received after our sighting of the UFO the evening before our Stargate.

Dear Mr Glanville,

I am writing with reference to your recent report of an "unexplained" aerial sighting which you observed on 11 October 1996. The details of your report have been passed to this office, as we are the focal point within the Ministry of Defence for all matters relating to "unexplained" aerial sightings of "UFOs".

First perhaps it would be useful if I were to explain the role that the Ministry of Defence has with respect of this subject. The Ministry of Defence examines any reports of "UFO" sightings it receives solely to establish whether what was seen might have some defence significance; namely is there any evidence that the UK Air Defence Region might have been compromised by a foreign hostile military threat, and to date no "UFO" sighting has revealed such evidence, we do not attempt to identify the precise nature of each sighting reported to us. We believe that down-to-earth explanations are available for most of these reported sightings, such as aircraft seen from unusual angles or natural phenomena.

In this particular instance we are not aware of any evidence which would indicate that a breach of the UK's air defence has occurred; we received no similar reports for 11 October, but have noted your report and would like to thank you for your interest. I have attached the addresses of some organisations you may wish to contact.

I hope this is helpful.

Yours sincerely,
Gaynor South

***

11th October 1996 - eve of the Stargate

The build up to our Stargate was enormous. The whole week was full of talk and preparation for this very special morning. We decided to meet at 8.00pm the night before.

Sleeping arrangements being made as most of the group were to stay overnight. We couldn't imagine what the night was going to bring and didn't dare to think about the following morning.

Leaving work that day the excitement was high.

"I'll do some last minute shopping," I said to David as I jumped into my car, followed by Jeff.

"I'll come," he said.

"I'll meet you both at the Tandoori after," David added.

"Dave, let Nick know what's happening," I shouted, sticking my head out of the car window, barely missing the oncoming traffic.

Normally our Friday treat at the end of a working week was a family get together. It was a time to relax and enjoy the delights of a lovely Nepalese meal, after which we would all descend on my lovely mum, putting our feet up and extending the evening into a sociable event. *But this night Jean had other plans and a different treat in store for us.*

Jeff and I went home to unload the shopping. Leaving Jeff on the drive, I ran across the garden to the house. Filled with great apprehension, I fumbled to unlock the back door, thinking all the time of the forthcoming event. Jeff struggled across carrying more bags than he should have done.

"Be careful, you might drop something," I moaned.

Finally the key twisted in the lock and I pushed the door open. I had barely put my foot over the threshold when Jeff yelled in my ear.

"Mum, look up over your head quick!"

Looking up, I saw the most wondrous sight: a very bright object shot across the sky with great speed like an arrow. There was no noise whatsoever. It left a vapour trail against the dark sky. We stood in stunned silence and awe, watching it closely as it disappeared into the night sky.

"A bloody UFO," I shouted.

"East to West," Jeff said, very precisely, adding that he had a very strong feeling that this UFO was a sign regarding our Stargate and not a coincidence!

Over the months, our group had become very sociable sometimes about 10 of us, so when we met, laughter was on the agenda. Falling through the door, they all gathered with great enthusiasm and excitement, armed with sleeping bags, overnight attire and, of course, alarm clocks, although we were not really expecting to sleep at all.

Jugs of water on the dining room table, the air filled with perfumed oils, candles lit - the room was in order to sit. The chairs neatly placed, each person had their own special place, as we believe it contains that person's energy. After telling everyone about our UFO experience, we settled down for the evening's séance.

Firstly, there was a beautiful prayer from John P who asked for love and protection for us all. Then we gave our thanks and support to Jean and all his unseen helpers. Our spirit guides were then called upon. We sat in silence meditating, connected in spirit throughout our circle.

Suddenly, I felt a strange being present in the room. It seemed to have searched around the entire group and came to me, filled my head and made it buzz. The buzzing seemed to say, this one is special - the mother. My head seemed to expand, like a pumpkin and with that it went from me. No! It did not leave the circle; it entered my sister. Suddenly and without warning, Dilys spoke in trance with spirit for the very first time and gave a full message!

The message she gave that night came through clearly.

Many souls that had been safely gathered in had been stolen on the night of the 10th Oct (1996). They had penetrated the sealed door and took the adjuras (souls) right from under our noses. The battle between the darkness and light, positive and negative, was in progress. The robbing of the souls was for the need of pure energy for the matrix, the eternal darkness, place of no return (Bhalore - Satan).

It's not like Mother: a place of endless love and choice that let the spirit return to earth, giving us all the chance to redeem our original sins through karma. This we know as reincarnation. This is the purpose of Jean's Stargate: to collect all the earth bound souls and return them back to Mother to enable them to have the freedom of choice. Mother - the place of spiritual birth, not only for us humans but for all God's creations/children.

"Be warned, on your guard, for many will come to steal your treasure."

The spirit spoke with a peculiar voice, Dilys' breathing became erratic. After confirming this, she went quiet for a moment then boomed out a second message. *This spirit is here for the protection of the Stargate and especially for Jeff.*

Immediately after these words fell from Dilys' lips, Jeff simply said, "Yes I know you. Your name is I'Ron. I was once with you in another life and form. We are old friends."

Jeff spoke with great tenderness and love for this being. You could actually feel the emotion filling the room. Old friends had been reunited in spirit from a great past somewhere in the Universe. I'Ron had come to protect and stand guard, recognising our great spiritual event in our earthly calendar and, of course, as Jeff in trance confirmed, all over the Universe. Millions upon millions of souls were being gathered in the name of God to be transported home. The fight was on and Mother must be the victor.

This night Jeff received the very first light symbol and named it I'ron (pronounced I-RON). Jeff experienced these "light symbols" frequently after this date. Headaches, sickness, and even diarrhoea would often accompany the birth of these beautiful signs, which could come at any time and in any place. They were some kind of alphabet for him only. He felt an intense sense of urgency to draw them on anything at hand - some would come at 3.00am, waking him up gently to engage him to draw the symbols.

On one occasion he grabbed an old shoebox from under his bed and drew some of his most beautiful spiritual signs. The bright white, light images would appear to him as if on a computer screen. As

I'Ron

Jeff's 1st Light symbol
Oct 11th 1996
Copyright Jeff Glanville

soon as the "light symbols" were drawn in a precise manner, correct and completed, he would then be left completely calm and in good health with no ill effect whatsoever.

We do believe these symbols have been given in friendship and love. Jeff has already revealed some of their meanings by way of meditation, *and the remaining symbols are to be unlocked at a future date when told and required (not illustrated in book).*

The ones displayed in this book are for spiritual awareness and Stargate only (pages VIII to XIII).

The evening progressed with great ease after I'Ron's departure. Many spirits came forth with thanks, knowledge, wisdom and love. The evening came to a close, but I'Ron was to become very special to us all throughout that year.

David, Dil, Lyn and I walked into the front garden, feeling the dew under our feet, smelling the night air and once again thanking Jean for bringing us all together in such a loving way to do his deed.

Standing on the ley lines with the landing strip in front of us, I remember David saying, "I think a space ship is going to land," making us all laugh. He liked his little joke, but it did make you stop and think. What should we expect?

"Feel the energy Dil," I said, gazing up to the rooftop, watching the tiny spiritual pin pricks of light rolling in and disappearing into the house. The gathering of sweet souls was still going on. Jean was working overtime. The spiritual light (the beam) was still shining bright in the darkness.

Trying to settle down for the night was very hard, but finally all was quiet. Dil and Lyn slept in the green room - our Italian lady's favourite. Leaving the bedroom door open, they watched the spiritual pinpricks of light making their way across the landing to the void well into the night. That night we all slept safe and sound, protected and loved, as some higher being was watching over us.

The time to test and prove our love, faith and, above all, our trust in them was approaching.

Holy Day has arrived
To bring home Mother's pride
Lost and lonely souls in the night
No one matter who
It is justified, correct and right
Before they meet thine maker
They will reflect and regret
Their earthy sins
That will be washed away with the heavenly light.

Thelma Glanville

CHAPTER 22
STARGATE 12TH OCTOBER 1996

The morning had arrived at last! Dil and Lyn were awakened by the sound of chuffing, clanging and hoots. A noisy train alarm belonging to Jeff had been placed in their bedroom but, may I add, not by human hand! What laughs - as though they needed an alarm call that morning.

A light breakfast laid out on the table was eaten with great gusto. I of course was up first at 6.30am. This was certainly a test for me, as I am always the last one to hold onto the bedcovers. I milled around dressing, talking, washing, eating and waiting for the others to arrive, especially John the gardener. John the gardener had been told the layout and standing positions of our circle on that special day by spirit. Finally everyone gathered, well before 7.15am.

We took up our allotted positions, which encircled the house and front garden, incorporating the kitchen and the den and covering the two entrances from the gym. We were placed so each person could see his neighbour. This was to enable us to pass the energy around. We had two extra guests that morning who had requested to be present. The first one was Albert, Heather's husband, who is now a great and valuable member.

The other person attending was Dr. Frances from London, the spiritual lady who practises the art of regressions and who had witnessed my first ever ET experience that afternoon, after breaching the void door. Apparently, she had experienced similar 'gateways', which had opened in an unnamed place in Morocco.

There she sat holding hands with Gina in the kitchen, facing the other door to the gym. Gina was allowed to sit as she had been unwell for a long while. At the foot of this door, Jean had placed a small iron fender, giving a bed for Ben's blanket, neatly rolled up and kept firmly in place with his collar. This was symbolic to us - I could imagine my lovely dog Ben sitting there waiting for the children

Ben passed:- Monday 15th July 1996.
Bens blanket & collar at the foot of the 2nd door to gym before Stargate, put there by spirit. Placed in a firegrate fender.

to pass by.

Outside the kitchen window, Jeff and Dil stood by the open garden gate, where both were able to look in at Gina and Francis. I was next, looking at the gym and the statue of the monk who still stood proudly on my gold leaf stand following that rainy night, but was now fully uncovered for all to see.

Next in the circle were Heather, Lyn, John P and Albert who were all standing well into the front garden and on the runway. They were all looking towards the house. David was right outside the window of the den, looking through to John the gardener who was standing in the den, opposite the door to the gym to complete our circle.

Bending our heads, we prayed together, waiting for the energy to build. The morning was bright and clear. The noise from the traffic and people going to work was extremely loud, but we were screened by the very high trees and although it was autumn there were some leaves on the branches to save our blushes from the people on the No 9 bus. Through all this we could still hear the birds singing.

Arms outstretched we waited and meditated. On the previous night, John the gardener had stressed that the circle should not be broken, as the energy would drop, closing the window or gateway to the spirit world, thus trapping the souls once again on earth. There was also the danger of Bhalore's robbers, who I believed were still lurking. Strong and dedicated we all stood together.

Sunrise 7.15am - the time was here. The energy was mounting - the tingles, the trance-like state upon us.

I spoke out loud: "All yee sinners go into the light." Yet I was a monk speaking to monks. I saw monks lining up. Suddenly, a surge of great power pounded through the circle pushing Jeff towards the iron garden gate. Stopping his fall, he held on with one hand, crushing a part of the formation of the gate structure with his power. It seemed that some outsider was trying to take control and break up the circle.

Immediately Dilys took control. I'Ron emerged just like my Jean would in the hour of need. Like a police escort he offered Jeff his protection and corrected the breach in the circle. All was protected and we were allowed to proceed.

As mentioned, Lyn was standing next to John P in the front garden on the spiritual runway. Lyn had experienced some strange phenomena at her dad's bedside at the moment of death. She saw his spirit leave his body; this experience she kept locked in heart until she opened up to me. To share such a private and heart moving emotion was wonderful for both of us.

This morning, Lyn was to receive another wonderful but heart-wrenching paranormal experience. Meditating and fully involved, she stood there until floods of emotional tears fell.

D-Day celebrations, when all old soldiers lined up and gently but proudly marched in line to the music of the band in honour of their lost comrades in the war.

This is what she described, but Lyn's soldiers were a mixture of children, men and women of all ages, from all walks of life and different eras in time - all happy and excited, but all in soldier order.

At the head of the line was our sweet Jean, their saviour, leading them to Jacob's Ladder - the face of an angel.

"I have been reborn to do this deed. I will take them out. I will lead them this time. FOLLOW ME. FOLLOW ME."

Some of the monks from the garden were being held back for some unknown reason. Perhaps it was not their time to return to paradise and they still had earthly spiritual duties to perform.

The wonderful children all individually touched Lyn's hand and gave thanks as they swept by. With this she wept like she had never done before. She threw off her shoes to give her the sensation of the earth beneath her feet - reality was required. She simply wanted to go with them, but she knew this was not possible.

At this point a fine mist seemed to fill the garden and very fine rain fell, like silicone, oily to the touch. Was this the hand of Jean touching us all with his love and thanks?

Lyn's eyes, still filled with tears, fixed upon Jean and his souls descending upwards and into a great, soft, loving, white light - climbing the ladder - the steps leading to Heaven Mother/God and sweeping away all their tears, Jean's earthly books were placed neatly at the bottom of the ladder - no longer required. The great mysteries of life were to be unfolded to him elsewhere.

The mist cleared and Lyn's eyes fell upon our tall Leylandii tree at the end of the runway. There, at the very top, the most magnificent butterfly came to rest, its wings fully expanded showing its full splendour. One of God's creatures was giving us a sign of completeness: the metamorphosis, looking back from whence it came, growing into something beautiful, becoming one with the Flower, becoming one with God, soaring up into heavens. Up! Up! Up! Home at last. The circle of life to death to everlasting life.

The air fell still and silent; not even a bird was to be heard. There was even a mysterious lull in the traffic. The autumn morning sun was now streaming through the trees, filling our hearts with peace, love and contentment. Still standing tall all in our places, we waited until the very end.

Gina, Francis and John the gardener, who had sat and stood in the house on this special day, witnessed the doors to the gym gently

NICKS VOID DOOR HAD ALSO OPENED UP TO RELEASE ENERGY.

open with the flow of the pure energy releasing all the souls gathered up by our sweet Jean.

Their hearts and eyes welled up with love, especially for the children. They saw them all walking hand in hand into the garden in a neat orderly line, smiling and happy, slightly nervous with excitement like it was their first day at school, fussing and patting our Ben as they passed by who returned their affection.

A call from John the gardener brought us all rushing into the house. The gym room of course was the first room to be inspected.

Gently we entered gazing in with great apprehension, still feeling the great love that had been bestowed upon us.

The room was now just a gym room. The beer bottles had gone and a curtain tie back had been placed on the equipment, representing a rainbow, as confirmed by spirit and of course the bench that had been balanced for weeks had now been lowered. Looking and touching with great excitement, we almost forgot the most important thing we placed there before the room had been sealed: the book we'd left for Jean to enter all the names.

There it sat, still on the pec seat with the pencil at its side, just an ordinary lined exercise book. There, written in pencil - a message. It looked like Hieroglyphics, Egyptian symbols or even ancient Hebrew. Picking up the book we held it to our hearts: Jean's message to us - not written by human hand. One day, when the time is right, we will fully understand the symbols.

The whole room had been swept clean. The beer bottles were simply gone. No evidence at all was left in the deep pile carpet where they had been standing for weeks. They'd gone into another dimension, just like my carriage clock on that very first day of our beginning.

All the souls had departed except for some of the earthbound monks. The whole house had become light and clear like mountain air. It was finally over. *Dimensional Gateway*

*Jean's symbols left in excercise
book after Stargate*

ON REFLECTION JEAN'S FIRST SYMBOL LOOKS LIKE ONE OF JEFF'S SPIRITUAL SIGNS. THE RAINBOW REPRESENTS THE COLOURS OF THE SPIRIT WORLD.

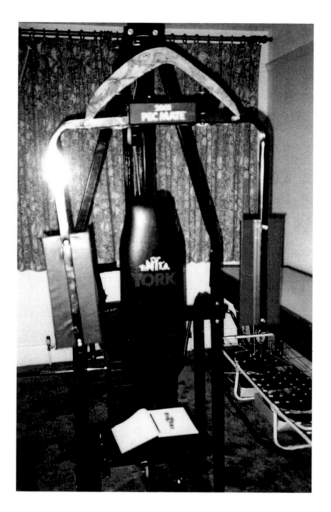

*Found when Stargate had finished, doors open for us
all to see. (Picture with rainbow & curtain tie)
Symbols written in the book by Jean and left in the gym room
on Peck seat. (Waiting room) Resealed by David (den door)
after breach by Bhlalore who came to steal souls.*

Jean-Louis

By candle light
He studied so deep
To enlighten his mind
To find knowledge and to reap
The ancient world of secrets
To find the answers that he seeked
His precious books and scrolls, oh so neat
Kept within his reach
Mind and heart so dedicated to one's life achievement
Yet finding himself lost in his own bereavement
Awaking to this fact
He came back
To enter our earthly plane in spiritual form
To lead, to save, through his heavenly gate
To redeem himself and remind us all
To wake up before it's too late.
To save our previous world today
For our spiritual way.

Thelma Glanville

Written to one who understands after the Stargate

24th October 1996

Dear Ernie,

Thanks for your letter, sorry for the delay in replying, but things have been hectic. I found your letter most exciting and I was pleased to find someone that understands what we are experiencing.

Just to recap, we confirmed the situation we found ourselves in when we met you at the UFO meeting. Since May this year, we have been visited - through trance of course by many spirits. A story unfolded before our very eyes, we have many tapes/photos to bear witness to this event. Through trance and signs in the house the date October 12th at 7.15am became quite evident. Approximately three weeks before this date our gym and small roof void over this room became sealed and taboo signs were put over the doors.

We came to the UFO meeting because when I was in trance on the previous Sunday I received a message from an 'ET'. I knew it was different as it came to me 'in my head' and not through the body (this was not taped as it took us by surprise.) At the UFO meeting, on hearing you, we understood the connection between the spirit world and ET's. Since then we have received many messages from them and even on the Friday the 11th at approximately 7.25pm we had a UFO pass over the house from east to west. The object was witnessed by my son Jeff and myself. It was a very bright light that shot over the house (like from a gun) that left a light trail in the sky for a few seconds. It shook us, as we had never seen a UFO before (IT WAS NOT A SHOOTING STAR). That night our circle gathered to give up love for the coming event and we received an ET, which confirmed the UFO visit (taped). It was received through my sister Dilys, who as always had trouble in talking in trance, but this evening she did not stop (I mean all night until the next day). She came through speaking to us all about the morning of the twelfth, as by this time we understood that we had a porthole or Stargate that many spirits were to pass through to Mother.

The expression Mother was given to us in trance through Jeff. When this ET came through that evening it said to my son Jeff that he knew him and that they were as "one" and would unlock his memory to the past. This, my son understood and immediately named this ET I'Ron and at that time (unknown to us all) Jeff was receiving symbols in his head which he had only just informed us of that evening. He has now drawn these and also the ones he received when speaking again to I'Ron after our meeting on Oct 11th Friday (Pre-Stargate) Sat 12th Oct. The name I'Ron came to my son in his head in a very loud scream that's the only way he could describe it and he translated it as I'Ron.

The morning of the twelfth. Through trance we were told to form a circle within the house and outside which we did. The spirits took an hour to go through the gate. We all received different experiences, which we have recorded. It seemed that not all the spirits passed over for some reason. The sealed doors opened up on their own accord and certain items (previously moved by the spirits moved back). The house is now very quiet and peaceful for the time being,

I'Ron's visit. We worked out the reason for his visit as on the Thursday night at approximately 7.30pm of October 10th Jeff was sitting in the room next to the gym (sealed door) when the door became slightly ajar. He went into a trance but was choking and sweating with fear. I ran into the room and immediately closed and held the door. My husband actually tied up the door. We were all very upset that this had happened but did not know why as none of us had any thoughts on the subject at all.

It was only when I'Ron came to us on Friday the 11th that all was revealed. Some of the spirits, which had been gathering within the room, had been stolen or deceived by other forces or aliens. It was only then we realised that I'Ron had been called upon for protection of the Stargate.

On the door's opening on the morning of the twelfth we checked the notebook which we had left in the gym hoping for a message but not really expecting one. To our surprise we found written in pencil symbols as per copy enclosed. Also enclosed Jeff's symbols from I'Ron. We would appreciate your comments on these.
Ernie as I am writing this letter to you, I am thinking is this really happening? Talking to ETs and my son being "as one" with I'Ron... what does it all mean for the future?

Throughout this ordeal we have had a very strong influence of Egypt and the Pyramids. We also got the impression that the Egyptians knew the secret of the shortcut back to Mother being the spirit world.
As I previously stated Ernie we have plenty of evidence (tapes, drawings, etc). If you can make any sense out of all this as to why we have be chosen. We would appreciate your views.

Many thanks and best wishes.

Yours Sincerely
Thelma and Co.

Onwards and forward like soldiers, are we
Fighting for goodness and honesty
Show the way for ones who are lost
To open up what is locked.
Minds and hearts connected you see
Will change the whole of humanity
So let us hope, let us pray for everyone this very day

Thelma Glanville

CHAPTER 23
DOMINIC - HIGHER REALM SPIRIT

The day of the Stargate will stay in our hearts forever, especially for Lyn, for I know how deeply she felt their love. I wish she could come to love herself and find her own peace.

Lyn and I knew that some of the monks had stayed behind, being held back for an important task on this earth, their space in time. In the weeks that followed, our group met in the normal manner: meeting in love and harmony, raising the vibrations to receive spirits who urged us all to go forth together. Receiving positive signs around the house, we all felt very well and uplifted.

Since the Stargate, we have channelled spirits from the higher realm. Dominic, a monk of great love and guidance for us all, told us of a pilgrimage that would come to us. He told us that our place in time had become holy, a place of safety, a time to prepare and to keep vigilant, a time of meditation, and to look within ourselves, as we are all our own temples:

"He all who gathers here in the love and light shall be remembered for thou art walking and talking to thine creator." **Spirit Dominic**

We are all beings of light, creations of God. He loves, cherishes and knows each time we falter along our spiritual pathway. He forgives us each time and encourages us to go forth with freedom of choice.

This reminds me of my bracelet used by the spirits each time we had done well in our rescue work. It has five interwoven rings - an inexpensive piece of jewellery. Each time, it would be whisked away and reappeared, set out in the most beautiful formation. The visiting spirits told us that this represented:

God known as Mother / God

1. Peace
2. Love
3. Harmony
4. Understanding
5. Knowledge

The circle of life and death to everlasting life. In the words of Aesop, "In union there is strength."

Thelmas bracelets.
Symbolic to represent the circle of life.

Looking back and recalling that first day in the garden, it's been difficult to remember each individual event. These things happen so fast and furiously. Trying to remember the many incidents that happened to my family and I during that period would only cloud the real purpose of that special visit on that very first day: for Jean, the saviour of the lost souls, to shine. Jean and his Stargate: the way back to Mother/God.

It's quite obvious that our story and spiritual experiences will go on, as Jean is preparing us for future spiritual works.

Thelma channelling Jean in trance
Second Stargate (Opening of Gateway)
12th of May at 9.30pm 1998

Further Vital Rescue Work Required by Jean-Louis – 2nd Stargate

I feel I must explain that our 'spiritual dimension gateway' was re-opened once again by Jean-Louis to carry out vital rescue work on Tues 12th May 1998 at 9.30pm.

Our group was most surprised when he came through within our spiritual gathering. Although, on arriving home that evening and finding the items left on the table – 'fish ordainments and fish nets', we knew something 'special' was on the way.

So when Jean came through in trance, we knew rescue work was required once again and the gateway was open.

As you will read through my channelling you will 'gleam out' that the souls came, and I quote, "as one comes from the water that floats from the depths", and I quote, "you are the net, you are catching them".

I do remember before that evening, he gave me the following message:-

I have a ditty here and sound
To prove you I am still around
Loud and sure you call my name to rally everyone to be saved
So don't you worry no more

For you are all in my arms for I am Jean
Call me in your hour of need
From others that will try to up heave
So my darlings came to me
For you know I love thee
Jean

Thelma (channelling Jean): All individual ones. The path has been stony, the path has been rough for them. Make them welcome to your circle they are lost souls coming home to Mother. Give them your love on the way, open the doors for them. Shine the light for them for they are Mother's children coming home again, once again. Follow them as far you can. Behind them push them gently; direct them to the light. For you are their helpers, you are their salvation, you have been chosen for this deed on this earth. Gather together with love and the harmony for these poor unfortunate souls. You will meet them one by one. You will know them. You will know their names, you will know where they come from and you will know of their loss. But they will gain what they have lost through you. You must be honoured, very honoured to do this deed that it is set before you. Your heart's open, the love pouring through. Let them stay awhile with you then release them through. Some will be ok for you to handle, some will not. Some will be very hard for you, enormous task we ask of you but you are protected you are well loved and we are with you all the way. We shall not let you down, you shall not let us down, and you will not let them down. For I know you are good honest souls on this earth. This gate is open, opened wide, the love is pure and simple. It is all, it is all, and love is all. All we have to give benefit from this love for the wisdom it holds, the knowledge it holds for you. You on this earth, the time will come when you will know why, you will know why all this is necessary. Do not ask too many unnecessary questions, ask the questions that are near to your heart and will help you to do this deed. The gates are wide open and the love I can feel. I have an enormous smile for you all.

(Thelma chants.)
Thelma: Greeting my friends to you all this evening. I have been

chosen this evening to be with you, especially you few this evening.

(David enquires as to whom is speaking.)
(Thelma chants.)
(Silence.)
(Two souls enter. A snake like creature wants to linger for a while. Young girl in distress, falling water, blood, death - no names as yet.)
Thelma: THE WAITING ROOM, THE WAITING ROOM, IT'S THE WAITING ROOM ALL OVER AGAIN.

(Jean enters again.)

Thelma: One by one they will come, one by one they will enter. They will come here to the safe place. It is most welcoming for them, the light is shining for them. They will come in and sing their songs to you. They will pour their troubles out to you, they will give you their names, let you know who they are in good time. This is their waiting room, this is their waiting room, and this is theirs. Their space in time, their space in time, ooh, ooh, so much love is here for them. The easy ones will come in at first, opening like a flower in front of me, each one is the petal, each one forms the flower. Does my heart good to welcome them here this evening.

Dave: Is this Jean?

Thelma: Yes

(All laugh.)
Thelma: Here again at long last is where my heart is!

Dave and Heather: Is the Stargate to be in the dining room?

Thelma: Their space in time!

(Group passes the light around. Dilys sees a queue of souls and queries this as they are outside the circle looking in.)

Jean: It has started, filtering through has started. Be prepared for the gates are opened, for the easy ones will come at first. They will come back and speak to you when their memory has passed of their passing.

(It gets very cold in the room and the group talks of the light.)

Jean: Beacon is up, be happy my children for you are in full flight this evening, "you are the net, you are catching them."

David: Like moths to the light.

Jean: You will contain them for the while until it's time to go. You will make a harbour for them, a safe harbour for these souls. This is right, this is how it should be, this is wonderful. They will filter through now one by one. When they come with strange stories strange beings may come through but they are all going home to Mother eventually.

David: Are some not in our likeness?

Jean: They will be when they come to you, they will change, they will enter from the darkness to the light, their whole being will change, light changes you, transforms you, this is good. Keep welcoming them, tell them you are here, do your collection now, collection has started, time is now right, gather, gather them in. Be prepared for the ones that will fight against what you have to offer them. There will be some difficult ones that do not want to come in from the darkness.

Heather: Why are they here?

Jean: Must go in and get them while Bhalore is away. You have to delve into their world, pluck them from the darkness. The ones... some will come through, some will hover half way through, in and out, you will have to pluck them through. These are the difficult ones.

David: Once in, no going back.

Jean: I can see the light, you can see the light. The ones to be rescued will come "as one comes from the water that floats from the depths" to the top, they suddenly appear and come in. The queue you see is something completely different, they are the ones that are outside looking in that do not need to come into the waiting room, they are not required. Some will come from the peashooter, they will be expelled through the peashooter.

(The group asks what a peashooter is.)

Jean: Needs to be more in the group to receive them, as they will enter. Children, whoever you receive, whatever they have done, they are all God's children, they are all God's children. Forgive them, cherish them, love them for they come to you for their salvation. And I thank you so much I love you so much.

(Message ends from Jean.)

The dimensional gateway closes

***

Our account of the events that brought us into the light may have a conclusion for now, but there will be no real ending until the good people of this earth spiritually awake and realise the coming of the new era.

A new life begins, we must prepare ourselves morally and spiritually and time is short! As our sweet Jean shouted out to rescue the lost souls: "Wake up you sweet people before it's too late!"

We are in the midst of a dimensional shift that will affect us all. This we have experienced as have other spiritual groups, all over the world. It's up to us all to find a way. We ignore the signs at our peril.

> We will either find a way or make one.
> **Hannibal**

The year of 1996 was not only been a period of enlightenment, but one of great spiritual change. These changes have brought about a whole new concept of thinking and understanding. A window has been opened letting in fresh air, freedom and truth. A light in the darkness has shone for my family and I. The spiritual/ET world does exist and help for mankind is at hand and there is a simple message:

"Love thy neighbour for time is short, bring peace and harmony and stop destroying the world, our beautiful planet a jewel in the universe, created by Mother/God. Created for our learning process that fits in with the whole concept of creation."

These lessons learned and the lost spiritual knowledge regained through the choices we have been given - all these things are taken back to Mother through the passing over in spirit. Mother is our womb where mankind is born in spirit: a place of total love, understanding and choice. Yes, choice!

I do believe when you return to Mother in spirit you have a choice to be reborn either into this world or the universe for your Karma. Returning to this earth for a period of further learning, as a beggar or a king, and gaining experience, good or bad, will only enable the spirit world to be enhanced by adding the knowledge gained to her memory banks. The system of things must survive at all costs otherwise mankind will suffer the consequences.

These warning signs have not only been displayed to us visually with the help of our dimensional friends in time and space, but many messages are now being received from the spirit realm (otherwise known as channelling). We are now entering a new horizon/dimension and must prepare ourselves spiritually and raise our vibrations to unlock our sub-conscious minds to gain the old knowledge we have lost through the centuries, as this is necessary for our survival as a human race.

Remember, we only have one world, one earthly home and one human race - it's about time we all realised this fact before it's too late!

Open up your heart we have only just begun...

Channelled 26th June 2002:

> *Ding dong the bell rings*
> *For mankind to come on in*
> *To start anew to bring the news*
> *For thou art coming to save you all bring me your good bring me your bad*
> *For I am going to renew for a new beginning*

Communication from our spirit being named Q (message received via spiritual table at home):

> *Your world has a right to defend itself so may the dust of exploded beliefs make a fine sunset.*

Wisdom of the Higher Extraterrestrials

The heart connected to the mind is awesome and will change the whole of humanity.

Within the pages of my account and the 'build-up' of Jean's Stargate, it became apparent that an ET connection was involved in our 'full blown spiritual awakening'.

When and how did we three connect with ET's? This was the big question that hung over Jeff, Dil and me (Thelma). Now through regression sessions it has become quite clear that 'time loss and abduction' had taken place on my 49th Birthday (13th of May 1995) the very first day on a holiday in Florida USA, for the three of us. Also it was revealed that my son Jeff had been abducted from the age of five. May be a 2nd book in the near future to document the ongoing events in our lives. Dilys is the only reluctant one to resist all attempts to be regressed, so her account is yet to be aired. We have come to the conclusion that we have been programmed differently to channel their messages. Yet when sitting in a 'closed spiritual circle' we form as one.

We have received many messages but one message is very clear to us all, the nations of this world must unite spiritually before it's too late.

References from Dr Noel Huntley Phd

"One might say the ET connection represents man's salvation on this plant. To connect with extra-terrestrials is an intrinsic part of man's evolution or ascension. – ETs and evolution are not separate. True evolution is accompanied by releasing right-brain activity and by the opening of the heart centre that automatically brings in perception and awareness of ETs. The right-brained/heart perception is capable of knowing by resonance with the universe, creating instantaneous understanding of even holistic patterns of information without the left- brained (mental) breakdown analysis. Over the years, many individuals have related wisdom shared with them during a contact experience with the higher Extraterrestrials (ETs). Most of those forms of contact involve either a physical contact or a meeting of the awareness as in mind to mind contact. We find in paranormal literature, two major categories of physical contact experiences - those that are overwhelming fearful and negative and those which can be considered positive. The negative experiences are usually related to the so called "abduction" scenario, characterised by fear, forced examinations, medical procedures, lost time and lost memory. In contrast, contact with positive ETs usually leaves a feeling of blissful well being and often involves the feeling of a flow of love and understanding from the ET. However even positive ET experiences can prove to be fearful for the person who has no context of understanding to make sense of them, and these experiences are often repressed only to be uncovered years later through hypnotic regression. Those who have made contact with positive ETs are often given a message of wisdom to pass along to the remainder of humanity.

Besides direct contact, another source of wisdom from higher ETs is through the phenomenon of channeling, or inner contact. Many individuals who have centered their awareness in the inner self through meditation or the quieting of the active mind, have experienced a soul to soul contact with higher ET beings. They may have intentionally volunteered themselves to be conduits for this type of communication, or they may have been selected for the purity and accuracy of the channel. In either case, people have recorded the thoughts and concepts that have come through such communication, passing them along to the rest of humanity.

ET wisdom gained both by direct contact and by conceptual transfer through selected individuals (channeling)."

Source: www.cosmicharmony.com/LightWorkers/ETWisdom/ETWisdom.htm

The Coming of Our Salvation

To you!
The people of this earth
Listen carefully while I tell my tale
Of dark days ahead
And things you might dread
Bury your head - if you may
In deep sand or even clay
If don't you want to hear
The truth that will be told - so clear!
The Day of Judgment is at hand
In the words of Elijah
Men will cast a shadow over this land
The downcast will rise to higher heights
Seek the light for guidance and ask for might
From GOD'S kingdom will come a messenger
In many languages the truth shall be - shouted!
To all corners of this land - it will be told
From mosques and temples of this world
As it was told in days of old
Before the first 'coming'
Gather the lilies of the field
Before they turn to dust
And scattered to the Four Winds
If not plucked - all will be lost - this is a must!
For these are the children of the future
That has come into the light
To conquer all on - HIS - terrible night!
He who is faithfull to the end
Shall inherit all what he sends
To stand against the powers of this corrupt system
Shall reap much more then thou art been given
So my children don't despair
People who come and go
Will not be there
To see the glory of your GOD'S triumph over man's deception.

Thelma Glanville

References

1. "Marianne Moore." AZQuotes.com. Wind and Fly LTD, 2017. 21 June 2017.
   www.azquotes.com/author/10340-Marianne_Moore

2. "Howard Zinn." Quotationsbook.com. 21 June 2017.
   www.quotationsbook.com/quote/854/

3. "Anais Nin Quotes" brainyquote.com. 27 June 2017.
   www.brainyquote.com/quotes/quotes/a/
   anaisnin131904.html

4. DR Noel Huntley Wisdom of the Phd. Higher Extra-terrestrials

Copies of The Why Files video can be purchased by request.

THE LOST DOCUMENT OF `Q`

On the arrival of our spirit called `Q` and the important messages received, investigation was required and to our amazement we found a document named `Q Source`

`Q` source (sometimes referred to as `Q` document or simply `Q`) comes from the German Quelle, which means `source`.

It is a hypothetical textual source for the Gospel of Matthews and Gospel of Luke.

`Q` is defined as the `common` material found in Matthew and Luke but not Mark.

This ancient text supposedly contained for logia or quotations from Jesus.

However the existence of a highly treasured dominical document, being omitted from all the early Church catalogs and going unmentioned by all the fathers of the early Church, remains one of the great conundrums of modern Biblical scholarship.

It is believed that some of the more notable portions of the New Testament are believed to have originated in `Q`.

Definitions

adgerate

Latin

Verb

adgerāte

1. Second-person plural present active imperative of adgerō

"Adgerate IS your soul"

My poems are inspired by spirit - since my awakening.

Ref:- Could Elijah be the next John the Baptist for the 2nd coming? <u>A Question to be answered.</u>

Humanity stands at the verge of an almighty change for you to transend this your structure tort must remain strong or you may faulter postitive thinking and actions smooth transition.

Q

Message from our spiritual guide Q - (via our spiritual table at home).

Our French carriage clock has never been returned to this very day,

Jean`s reminder to us all that `time is of the essence`.